TIMES TO REMEMBER
A CANADIAN PHOTO ALBUM

TIMES TO REMEMBER
A CANADIAN PHOTO ALBUM

KNOWLTON NASH

PHOTO EDITOR: MARJORIE HARRIS

KEY PORTER BOOKS

In association with CBC Enterprises

Canadian Cataloguing in Publication Data
Nash, Knowlton
   Times to remember

ISBN 1-55013-005-6

1. Canada – History – 20th century – Pictorial works*
I. Title.

FC600.N37   1986   971.06   C86-094497-2
F1034.2.N37 1986

Key Porter Books Limited
70 The Esplanade
Toronto, Ontario
Canada M5E 1R2

Design: Marie Bartholomew
Typesetting: Century Graphics & Typesetting
Printing and Binding: Metropole Litho Inc.
Printed and bound in Canada.

86 87 88 89 6 5 4 3 2 1

Contents

Fifty Years of Change

How we've changed in fifty years!

Today's Canadians are a very different breed from those of half a century ago. Through bust and boom, hot wars and cold wars, the changes we have gone through have been caught in moments frozen in time by that peripatetic contemporary historian, the news photographer.

News photography was around long before the mid-1930s, of course, but it is only since then that the still picture has become commonplace in the magazines and on the front pages. News pictures snapped on the run have captured a tear, a smile, a grimace, a moment that graphically reflects a major event or issue. As a result, we carry around in our minds more picture images of our time than our parents and grandparents ever could.

And what a time we've had! Modern news photography, born in the Depression, has let us see the tragedy of the "Hungry Thirties" and the triumph and sorrow of war. It has shown us the Dionne quintuplets, Canadian soldiers lying wounded on the beach at Dieppe and splashing ashore at Normandy, John Diefenbaker aquiver, the new Canadian flag, Expo 67, Trudeaumania, René Lévesque, and Terry Fox.

From bowler hats on our heads and spats on our shoes, to zoot suits, bikinis, mini-skirts, and jeans, from panhandling bums and marching soldiers to protesting hippies and jogging yuppies, the news photographer has captured the face of our country. Through the chaotic years of depression and war, through the postwar boom years and the tempestuous Diefenbaker-Pearson period, through the Trudeau years of pride and protest, and the uncertain last decade, we have seen ourselves change from a nation of wide-eyed innocents to a nation of sophisticated skeptics.

William Lyon Mackenzie King and Pierre Elliott Trudeau dominated the political landscape of our times: one seeking progress through conciliation, the other, progress through confrontation; one a prissy Victorian, the other flamboyantly Edwardian in style; one a supernaturalist, the other a rationalist; one narrow-minded, socially innocent, and moderately isolationist, the other broad-minded, sophisticated, and internationalist; but both seeking to reconcile our English and French heritages and to shape Canada into a unified, liberally progressive society. To a degree, they–and the other prime ministers since King–succeeded. Canadian society today is a rich, if sometimes confusing, mosaic. We have better education, better pay, and better health care, but we also have more crime, more divorce, and more suicide. For better or

---

In one of the most poignant photographs of the war, five-year-old Warren Bernard
runs after his father Jack, as the British Columbia Regiment marches through New Westminster, B.C., on its way to active service in Europe in 1940.

worse, families are smaller, most married women now work, and we don't go to church as much. We have "house-husbands" and single parent families.

Canadians in the 1930s were naively isolationist and unworried about war. Today we are keenly aware internationalists and fearful of nuclear obliteration. We are better informed and culturally richer, but we are still a culturally occupied country as American magazines, films, books, television, and music flood irresistibly across the border, and our sports become ever more American. With our rapidly growing economic ties with the United States, we are immeasurably more American and less British than we were half a century ago.

Canada has changed in other significant ways. Powered by C. D. Howe and his "Dollar A Year" men, our economy-and our personality-were transformed during the war and the postwar boom from essentially rural to overwhelmingly urban. In the 1930s most English-speaking Canadians were blindly unaware of the deep-rooted nationalism of Quebeckers and had a benignly neglectful affection for those quaint French-speaking members of the Canadian family. During the 1950s and 1960s, "quaint" became "outspoken," and after René Lévesque's referendum in 1980, better understood.

While Canada was built on the framework of Sir John A. Macdonald's National Dream-the railway-it is only since the 1930s that it has really been tied together as one nation by the Trans-Canada Highway, by air travel, by radio, by television, and by the shared experiences of depression, war, and boom times. Canadians know each other better today than ever before; if Newfoundlanders do not quite yet share with Yukoners Marshall McLuhan's vision of a "wired city," that time is getting closer.

At the same time, we define ourselves as different from our American neighbours. We stubbornly remain a people devoutly committed to the collective good and to the true-blue British North America Act credo of "Peace, Order, and Good Government" rather than to the more adventuresome, individualistic American Constitution philosophy of "Life, Liberty, and the Pursuit of Happiness."

The Americanization of Canada may continue apace in things material, but in things spiritual, we remain as we always have been: more comfortable with compromise than confrontation; more self-effacing and self-critical, less daring and less boastful than our American neighbours. Canadians always worry about a "rainy day" and demand more government social protection than do Americans. In fact, we have built a social safety net for old age, unemployment, health, and a host of other worries that would astound the Canadian of the 1930s.

We still envy others, but others envy us: our lifestyle, our space, our resources. We think we lack self-confidence, but the rest of the world thinks we are the ideal bridge between the snobbish English and the brash Americans.

Typically, we have built a nation not through massive blood-letting as our neighbours did in the American Revolution and the Civil War, but through patient and often exasperating negotiations. In the United States, frustration has been the wet-nurse of violence, but here, frustration seems to have been the wet-nurse of Royal Commission investigations. We are with Montaigne in his thought that "we must learn to endure what we cannot avoid." Canadian history has been less dramatic and less scarring than American history, but it has made us the way we are. Basically, we are forced to admit, though intellectuals disdain it, yuppies laugh at it, writers ridicule it, and most of us don't quite believe it, that Canadians are, heaven help us, "nice." And we are nicer today than we were half a century ago because we have suffered and learned and grown.

Canadians, however, still stand up and salute authority. We obey the rules. Civil libertarians may ache over it, but if we feel it protects the collective good we tend to support the authorities, whoever they may be and, for the most part, no matter what they may do, even if it means crushing individual rights. Witness the wartime expulsion of Japanese Canadians from the west coast; the abrogation of civil rights in the Gouzenko Royal Commission investigation; the War Measures Act and its aberrant consequences; and the RCMP "dirty tricks" in blatant law-breaking. Canadians overwhelmingly supported the government in all cases.

Like any nation we have our strengths and our weaknesses. Our history is as filled with heroes and rascals, grasping politicians, noble visionaries and realists, events tragic and comic, occasions momentous and fleeting. Thanks to news pictures and to the intrepid photographers who took them, the people and happenings of the last fifty years are brought alive for us. Seeing them, and seeing ourselves, we realize the incredible journey we've taken together.

36-46
The Chaotic Years

We were flat broke with no hope.

The Hungry Thirties . . . The Dirty Thirties: drought and hot, sucking winds churned the Prairies into one giant dustbowl as the soil blew away and the grasshoppers gobbled up what was left.

In the cities, factories were empty, the unemployed flocked to soup kitchens, slept fitfully in hobo jungles on the city outskirts, and rode out of town atop railway box-cars in search of work. "Brother, can you spare a dime?" was a motto of the times.

Those who had jobs – in Toronto, a public school teacher started at $28 a week – could buy a roast of beef for Sunday for $1, a three-piece man's woollen suit at Eaton's for $9.98, and a broadcloth shirt for 84¢. A Ford automobile was less than $1,000 (or about nine months of that new teacher's salary) and a five-room big-city bungalow was $6,000. Some people carried a single light bulb from room to room, screwing it into empty sockets to save the cost of electricity and extra bulbs.

Tim Buck tried to exploit these hard times to promote his communist utopia, but it was the newly born CCF, or Co-operative Commonwealth Federation, that captured much more attention, especially in the west.

This was a time when political giants strode across the Canadian landscape: "Bible Bill" Aberhart of Alberta, Jimmy Gardiner of Saskatchewan, John Bracken of Manitoba, Mitch Hepburn of Ontario, "Le Chef," Maurice Duplessis of Quebec, and Angus L. Macdonald of Nova Scotia; and at the federal level, Mackenzie King, Ernest Lapointe, C. D. Howe, Brooke Claxton, Doug Abbott and "Chubby" Power. Love them or hate them, they were domineering political masters in sharp contrast to the hesitant political souls of today.

They had to be tough to deal with the soul-destroying economic ruin of the Depression years – years that saw the "On-to Ottawa March" of jobless trekking eastward to protest their lot at the capital, the violent Regina riots, and a particularly nasty event at the Vancouver Post Office that became known as "Bloody Sunday."

But these were the big events; for those who could afford small luxuries, everyday life in the 1930s had its simple pleasures. You could go to the neighbourhood movies on Saturday afternoons for ten cents and see a double feature, a Flash Gordon serial, a cartoon, and the newsreel. If you had a bit more to spend, movies like *Snow White and the Seven Dwarfs* were at the downtown theatres for twenty-five cents. Canadians sat glued to the radio to hear Foster Hewitt scream, "He shoots! . . . He scores!" and on Sunday nights at 7:00 to hear Jack Benny tell jokes and sell Jell-O. As the thirties ground on, escape from our painful economic reality came via the fantasy of "The Lux Radio Theatre" and Bert Pearl's "The Happy Gang" on CBC radio. We heard the punches of Joe Louis, the "Brown Bomber," the cracking bat of "Iron Man" Lou Gehrig, and we gobbled up everything we could read about the Dionne quints.

Kids rode on the running-boards of the family Ford; teenagers "necked" in the rumble seat. Milk, bread, ice, and coal were delivered by horse-drawn

---

Previous page: Prime Minister William Lyon Mackenzie King toured Nazi Germany in 1937. Like Britain's Neville Chamberlain, he hoped that war could be averted through appeasement and was blind to Hitler's true objectives.

wagons that clip-clopped along leafy streets. Superman comic books were all the rage with the younger set and Monopoly and Chinese Checkers were played at the family kitchen table. On rare nights out, a "mickey" of rye might be had surreptitiously under the table at the ten-cents-a-dance club.

An event that transfixed our pre-war nation was the dramatic "You Are There" reporting of the CBC's J. Frank Willis from the scene of the Moose River Mine disaster in a tiny Nova Scotia village. It was the beginning of live broadcast journalism in Canada, and it electrified the country for eleven days and ninety-nine broadcasts before two men and one body were brought out. News photographers were there, too, to capture the drama of this desperate rescue.

Throughout the late thirties, we were consumed by our economic agonies; we saw, but did not comprehend the death rattle of world peace. When this chaotic decade had begun, Hitler was on the march, the Japanese were raping China, and the world economy was a shambles. All this was eclipsed for us as we heard Edward VIII give up his throne for "the woman I love," and later as we exuberantly welcomed the new King George VI and Queen Elizabeth on their visit to Canada. We frowned on the "Mac Paps," those left-wing, idealistic young adventurers of the Mackenzie-Papineau Battalion fighting Franco in the Spanish Civil War. Ethiopia, Abyssinia, Sudetenland, Austria, Czechoslovakia, and even Poland seemed so very far away.

Prime Minister Mackenzie King spoke for most Canadians after the Munich conference sell-out to Hitler by gushing to that apostle of appeasement, British Prime Minister Neville Chamberlain, "The heart of Canada is rejoicing tonight." King had met Hitler in 1937 and said that he was "a simple sort of peasant," adding, "I am perfectly certain the Germans are not contemplating war ."

But the peasant was not so simple, and two years later we marched off to war singing "Roll Out the Barrel" and "We'll Hang Out Our Washing on the Siegfried Line". We had an army forty-five hundred strong, five three-inch mortars, twenty-nine bren guns, and sixteen tanks–a year before, we had had only two tanks.

We acquiesced in war; mostly indifferent, unaware, and somewhat reluctant. There was none of the jingoistic fervour that had accompanied the start of the First World War. The CBC news bulletin that Canada was formally at war came on Sunday, September 10, 1939, when announcer Austin Willis interrupted "Smoke Gets in Your Eyes" on a lunch-time music program from NBC to read a Canadian Press report. That done, the CBC went back to the NBC music show, picking up the strains of "Inka Dinka Doo."

On the home-front, as the war years rolled on, Victory Gardens sprang up in neighbourhood empty lots, students became summertime farmers, and children collected paper, metal cans, and balls of aluminum foil for the war effort while their older sisters and mothers knitted socks and sweaters for the boys overseas. Sugar, butter, coffee, and tea were rationed. We stirred yellow dye into margarine to make it look like butter. There were "Meatless Tuesdays" and "Meatless Fridays," and liquor was rationed–Ontarians were allowed twelve ounces a month. Many a car was stored in the garage on blocks "for the duration" when gas and parts became scarce.

In as unlikely a duo as history records, Shirley Temple and Mackenzie King teamed up to sell Victory Bonds. We danced to Mart Kenny and his Western Gentlemen, listened to Glenn Miller on our 78s, laughed at Wayne and Shuster, Edgar Bergen and Charlie McCarthy, thrilled at the bombing raid exploits of CBC radio's "L for Lanky," and hummed "White Christmas" and "When the Lights Go On Again." We also knew all about Spitfires, Hurricanes, and Lancaster bombers. We worried about spies and fifth columnists in Canada and were warned that "Loose Lips Sink Ships!" Following the Japanese attack on Pearl Harbor in December 1941, and spurred by racial prejudice and political and governmental cowardice, thousands of Japanese Canadians were torn from their west-coast homes and forced into the interior.

There were the "Zombies"–conscripted soldiers who refused to serve overseas–and there were CWACs and WRENs and WDs. Lorne Greene, with his "Voice of Doom," boomed out the war news from the CBC with strange place names that had meant nothing before but that now would be forever burned into our memories: Dunkirk, Dieppe, El Alamein, Stalingrad, Hong Kong, Normandy, Hiroshima. Canada's soldiers invaded Sicily, slogged through Italy, and liberated much of the Netherlands, and air ace Buzz Beurling and Victoria Cross winners such as Padre John Foote became national heroes. Our destroyers and corvettes escorted North Atlantic convoys and chased German submarines prowling around the St Lawrence River where the subs brought the war home by torpedoing twenty-three merchant ships.

At long last the good news came. Paris was free, the Rhine crossed, and Mussolini and Hitler were dead. So, alas, was Roosevelt. VE Day (for Victory in Europe) and VJ Day, (for Victory over Japan) saw dancing and kissing in the streets and we all felt that indescribable, whooshing sense of relief that it was all over. Peace at last, and Canada had come of age into a new nuclear world.

Right: Canada was badly hit during the Depression, with up to 30% of the labour force out of work. In this classic photograph, unemployed men sit beneath a billboard advertising Heinz Tomato Ketchup. Ironically, ketchup became a staple during the Dirty Thirties–mixed with hot water, it made a skimpy meal.

In 1935 thousands of desperate, unemployed men from British Columbia, Alberta, and Saskatchewan climbed aboard freight trains in an On-to-Ottawa protest trek. It ended in mass rioting in Regina on July 1 with one policeman killed, dozens of trekkers injured, and 130 arrested.

Vancouver police hop on the running boards of a squad car rushing to a riot at the city's post office. This was one of a series of riots that took place early in 1935 to protest conditions in the unemployment relief camps run by the Department of National Defence.

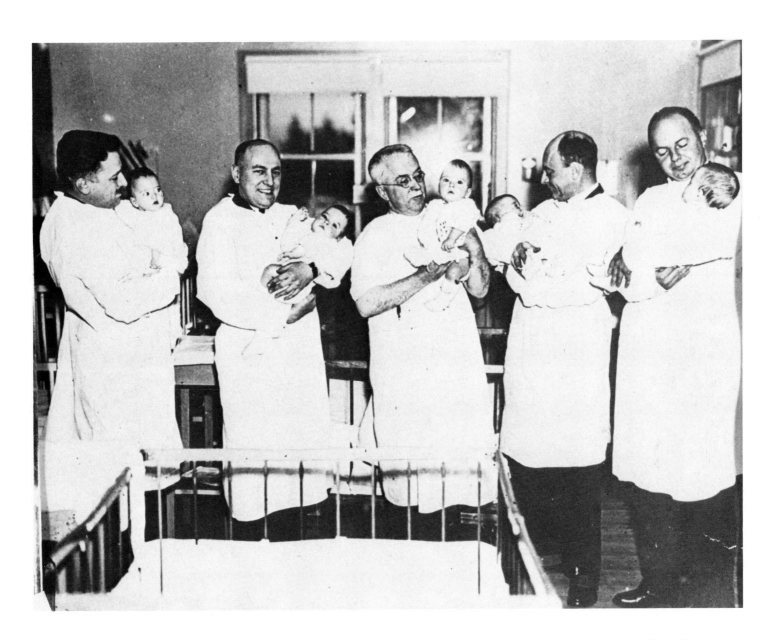

Left: As more and more Canadians became homeless during the Depression, shantytowns such as this one in Toronto became a frequent sight across the country. Amazingly, amid all this misfortune, a sense of humour could still prevail. One of the corrugated tin shacks in this picture has been given the dignified name of Hepburn House, undoubtedly dedicated to Mitch Hepburn, Ontario's premier.

Dr. Allan Roy Dafoe, centre, and Ontario Premier Mitch Hepburn, with the most famous babies of the 1930s, the Dionne quintuplets. Annette, Emilie, Yvonne, Cecile, and Marie, born on May 24, 1934, were the only quintuplets to that time to have survived more than a few days. Fearing private exploitation, the Ontario government made them wards of the state under the care of Dr. Dafoe. For the next nine years the government exploited them itself, allowing them to be used as a tourist attraction earning millions of dollars.

Above: C. D. Howe, Minister of Transport in Mackenzie King's government, boards a Lockheed 12 airplane on one of the first "dawn to dusk" transcontinental flights from Montreal to Vancouver, July 30, 1937. Howe was the minister responsible for the creation of Trans-Canada Airlines (later Air Canada) earlier that year.

Above right: Over the years, Nova Scotia has been devastated by many mining disasters. The one at the Moose River mine between April 12 and 23, 1936, was not one of the most tragic – only three men were trapped, two of whom survived – but it was famous, thanks to CBC reporter J. Frank Willis's live reports from the site of the disaster – the first such coverage in the history of Canadian radio news.

Below right: Marchers in Vancouver in 1937 walk under an ironic reminder of immediate needs – a marquee advertising the Kaufman-Hart musical, *You Can't Take It With You.* The desperate shortage of work caused many ordinary citizens to take to the streets in demonstrations.

Volunteers fighting in the Spanish Civil War in 1937 watch for enemy planes from their trenches. More than 1,200 Canadians went to Spain to defend the republican government against Francisco Franco and his Fascist allies, most as part of the Mackenzie-Papineau Battalion, named after the leaders of the rebellions of 1837. In 1939, as the civil war ended, only 600 Canadians survived to return home.

In a rare photograph, Dr. Norman Bethune (*far right*) stands with Dr. Richard Brown and soldiers of the Eighth Route Army in northern China, *circa* 1938. Bethune was a controversial surgeon, inventor, and political activist whose posthumous fame in Canada largely stemmed from his heroic status in the People's Republic of China. A champion of medical reform, he ran a mobile blood transfusion service in the Spanish Civil War and, later, participated in the beginnings of the Chinese Revolution.

King George VI and Queen Elizabeth leave Canada House in London on October 19, 1939, accompanied by High Commissioner Vincent Massey and Mrs. Massey. The royal visit to Canada in the spring of 1939 did much to unite a nation that was on the eve of world war.

Right: With the outbreak of war in 1939, garment factories across the nation were pressed into service. This entire factory was devoted to making uniforms for the Canadian Army.

While the war raged in Europe, the war effort continued at home in
Canada. Veronica Foster, known as the "Bren-gun Girl," appeared in
advertising and propaganda to promote women working in machinery
and armaments factories. After hours, she was a talented jitterbugger.

Pilots of Fighter Squadron No. 2, Royal Canadian Air Force, took initial flight training in Canada but completed it in England. Here, a group receives final flight instructions somewhere in England. The locations of British training camps were secret. This photograph was cleared for news release by the Canadian Censor in 1941.

Above left: A Japanese-Canadian internment camp community kitchen in Slocan City, B.C., in 1943. Over 20,000 Japanese Canadians were relocated under the War Measures Act. As the war drew to a close, with their land and possessions sold by the government, they were forced to choose between deportation to Japan or relocation east to other parts of Canada. Most chose to remain in Canada.

Below left: In December 1941, after the Japanese bombing of Pearl Harbor, the Canadian government ordered the confiscation of all Japanese-Canadian owned fishing vessels; in February 1942 it ordered the removal of all Japanese Canadians from an area within 160 kilometres of the Pacific coast. Although the RCMP and the military in Ottawa opposed this action, claiming the Japanese Canadians posed no danger, the government insisted that their presence on the coast was a threat to national security.

Above: Although the Canadian government entered the Second World War stating that it would not impose conscription for overseas service, by 1942 Prime Minister Mackenzie King bowed to increasing public pressure and announced a plebiscite to be held April 27, 1942. English Canada was overwhelmingly behind the idea of conscription and carried the vote for the nation even though almost 73 per cent of Quebec voted against it. Here the Rooney Club's dogcart promotes the "Yes" vote in Toronto.

Left: The dashing air ace, George Frederick (Buzz) Beurling, greets Prime Minister Mackenzie King on the steps of the Parliament Buildings, November 19, 1942. Though he destroyed 28 enemy aircraft in four months while serving with the RAF in Malta in 1942, he had difficulty with service discipline and was released in October 1944. In 1948, he joined the fledgling Israeli Air Force and died when the plane he was flying to Palestine crashed.

A group of corvettes sets sail from Halifax in 1941 to form the nucleus of the famed Newfoundland Escort Service. These Royal Canadian Navy ships valiantly guarded the convoys of merchant ships carrying the troops and supplies that were beleaguered Britain's lifeline during the dark days of the Battle of the Atlantic.

The Duke and Duchess of Windsor and their dogs at E.P. Ranch, Alberta, in 1941. The world was still shocked by the Duke's unprecedented abdication from the throne in 1936 in order to marry "the woman I love", twice-divorced American, Wallis Warfield Simpson. For the better part of the war (1940-45), he served as governor of the Bahamas. He would never live in England again.

Right: During the Second World War, Canada offered asylum to the princesses of the Netherlands. Princess Juliana arrived with her two daughters, Beatrix *(left)* and Irene *(right),* to spend the war years in Ottawa, where a third daughter, Margarethe, was born. The Canadian government declared the territory in which she was born Dutch to preserve her nationality.

This German photograph captures the tragedy of Dieppe, France, August 19, 1942, when an Allied force of almost 5,000 Canadians and 1,000 British Commandos attempted to land on French soil. The assault was met by an entrenched German force. Canadian troops suffered appalling casualties: almost 900 died and 1,900 were captured.

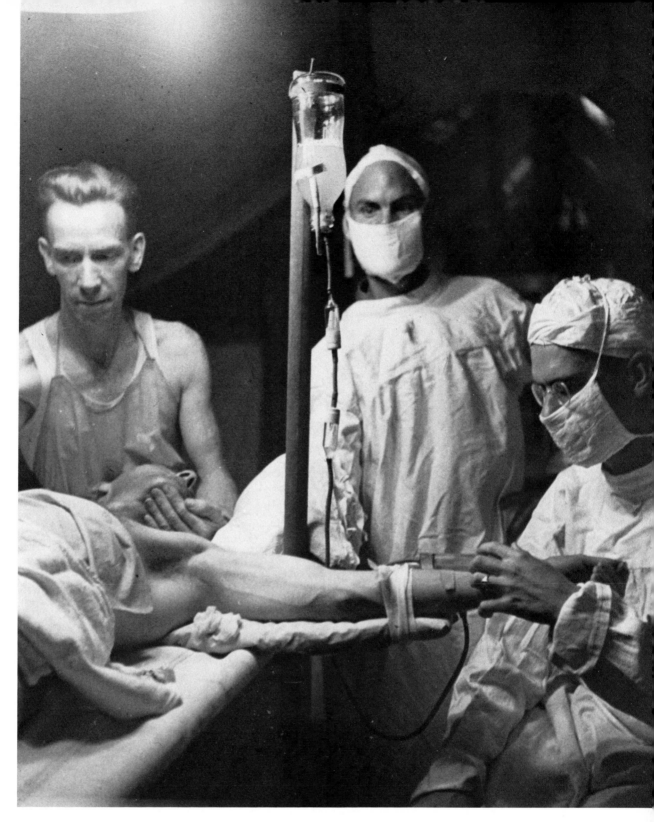

Plasma is given to a wounded soldier under the direction of Major F. G. Smith in El-Arrouch, Algeria, in September 1943. The medical corps performed an essential and often unsung service, providing medical care to the wounded under difficult field conditions.

Members of the Canadian Women's Army Corps take a cigarette break during a firefighting demonstration in London, England, on February 28, 1943. Three thousand CWACs were stationed in the U.K. and, starting in June 1944, select groups were dispatched to the continent as support staff for the invasion forces.

Right: A blind-folded, captured German submarine crewman is led ashore after his U-boat was sunk in the North Atlantic by ships of the Royal Canadian Navy. German submarines harried the convoys relentlessly, taking a heavy toll in the early days of the war. Escort warships fought grim battles, often of several days' duration, with the unseen German "wolf packs".

The Quebec Conference during August 1943 was the first of two top-level meetings held in Quebec City to plan Allied war strategy. In attendance were British Prime Minister Winston Churchill, American President Franklin Delano Roosevelt, and the Combined Chiefs of Staff. Though Canada was not officially represented, Mackenzie King attended as "host."

Right: General A.G.L. McNaughton addresses Canadian troops during the Sicilian campaign. McNaughton, as senior Canadian officer in the U.K. from 1939–1943, tried unsuccessfully to keep the Canadians together in one formation.

Previous pages: June 6, 1944, D-Day of the Normandy invasion. Troops of the North Nova Scotia Highlanders and the Highland Light Infantry of Canada wade ashore at Bernières-sur-Mer. Within two months, the Allies had liberated France.

Left: Canadian troops survey the damage in Caen, France, after a bloody battle following D-Day. The invasion was the first taste of combat for many soldiers.

Right: The lighter side of war: privates Vera Cartwright and Enid Powell pose with the young sergeants Frank Shuster *(left)* and Johnny Wayne *(middle)* at the Canadian Army Show, Bonville, France, on July 30, 1944. Wayne and Shuster became Canada's most famous stand-up comedy team.

Above: This poignant photograph of German children displaying a surrender flag at Sogel, Germany, in April 1945, captures the unsung toll of war. Following the collapse of the Nazi regime, thousands of orphaned children roamed the countryside aimlessly. Some were eventually reunited with their surviving family members; others ended up in refugee camps.

Above right: After heavy fighting, a small mixed force of 175 men from armoured and artillery units and the Argyll and Sutherland Highlanders of Canada under the command of Major D. V. Currie held St. Lambert-sur-Dives on August 19, 1944, under fierce attack from German troops attempting to escape from the Falaise pocket. Major Currie who was awarded the Victoria Cross for this battle, is at the left, supervising the round-up of German prisoners.

Below right: Members of the First Canadian Army make their way through crowds of cheering Dutch citizens during the liberation of Nazi-occupied Netherlands. Underground resistance led to mass executions and deportations and, of the approximately 112,000 Dutch Jews, 104,000 were deported to Poland and died in concentration camps. Forty years later, surviving Canadian veterans would return to Europe to relive their experiences and to be welcomed by those they had liberated.

AUSGANG
NUR IN
POW UNIFORM

As the war drew to a close, 34,354 German, Italian, and Japanese prisoners of war were in Canadian camps. Among them was this group in Sherbrooke, Quebec. To help fill the manpower gap between the end of the war and the repatriation of Canadian troops, about 22,000 of these men were put to work on farms and in the bush.

Right: Tommy Douglas led the Co-operative Commonwealth Federation to victory in Saskatchewan in 1944, becoming the head of the first socialist government in North America. He stands here at centre under a CCF billboard shortly after his election, with C. M. Fines *(left)* and Clarence Gillis *(right).* Premier of Saskatchewan and later, leader of the federal New Democratic Party, he was renowned for his political skills, his oratory, and his rapier wit. In introducing medicare, he changed the nature of medicine in Canada.

Above: Prime Minister Mackenzie King *(left foreground)* and Louis St. Laurent *(right foreground)* announce VE Day from San Francisco on May 8, 1945. During the war, 1,086,343 Canadian men and women served in the forces. Casualty figures were lower than they had been in the First World War, but 42,042 still lost their lives–a large number for a country with a population of only 10 million.

Above and below right: On May 8, 1945, as peace was declared, a convoy of troops was in Halifax harbour awaiting orders to sail for Europe. A cautious Naval Command and fearful city fathers agreed to confine all troops to their quarters and to ban the issue of alcohol. The result was the VE Day riots. The troops took over the town, looting over 150,000 bottles of alcohol and causing millions of dollars in damage to stores and houses.

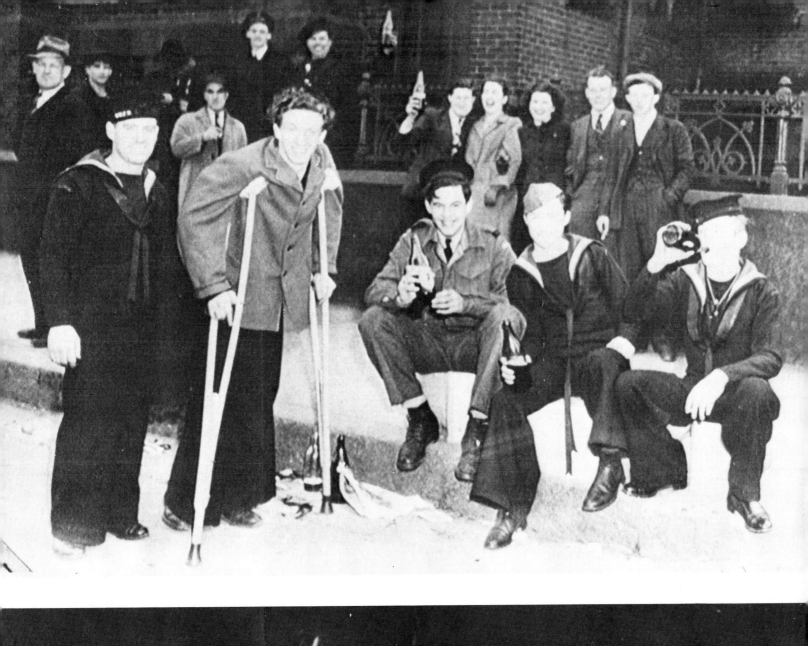

47-56
The Boom Years

The war killed the Depression, transformed Canada from a rural to an urban society, and set us off on one of the greatest booms in history.

We had little and we wanted a lot. We were over twelve million strong in 1945, with a voracious appetite for cars, clothes, houses, and all those things we hadn't been able to get during the war.

The boys came home from overseas, followed closely by their war brides and babies, and, a little later, a million "New Canadians." Polish, German, Italian, Dutch, and British accents suddenly flavoured our conversation, our lifestyle changed, and our taste buds were tantalized with garlic, spices, and new ways of cooking. Until then, we'd been content with boiled vegetables, boiled potatoes, and overcooked roast beef; our idea of an exotic foreign meal had been chop suey.

There was a business boom, a job boom, a baby boom, and a galloping gross national product. Oil was discovered in Alberta, the St Lawrence Seaway was begun, and Toronto built a subway. The suburbs exploded as Canadians left the farms and flooded into the cities, shopping centres sprang up, and every young wife in sight seemed to be pregnant and eyeing a five-room bungalow in a subdivision. Dr. Spock wrote our bible for raising all those baby-boomers.

Wash-tubs and washboards vanished, laundromats and electric dishwashers appeared, and new refrigerators meant we no longer needed to shove huge dripping blocks of ice into the icebox. We played canasta, laughed at Max Ferguson's "Rawhide" on radio–for which we no longer had to pay a $2.50 a year licence fee for the CBC–and, in late 1952, television arrived. People with TVs saw their popularity increase as the neighbours came in to watch "Howdy Doody" on their ten-inch black-and-white sets. In 1957, a panel program called "Front Page Challenge" began–it was still going thirty years later. A nickel bought a lemon Coke or a streetcar ride, and the old age pension was forty dollars a month for those over seventy.

As the "Fabulous Fifties" rolled on, everything was "cool." Men in Brylcreemed hair escorted women wearing Dior's "New Look" to downtown bars in many cities where you now could get a rye and ginger by the glass. They might hop into their "Bugs," the distinctive small Volkswagens, to drive to the big circus tent in Stratford to watch Shakespearean drama, or to see a performance by the newly professional Royal Winnipeg Ballet.

Canadians smoked and drank more than ever before, forgot Rita Hayworth and fell in love with Marilyn Monroe, ignored Clark Gable and idolized Gregory Peck. Bobby soxers in their sweaters, skirts, and loafers still swooned at the mellow crooning of the pencil-thin, gaunt-faced Frank Sinatra. We cheered as Barbara Ann Scott won the World Figure Skating and Olympic championships, and as Marilyn Bell swam across Lake Ontario. Our hockey heroes were Syl Apps and Maurice "Rocket" Richard.

But the real hero of the decade was C.D.Howe, the Liberal cabinet "Minister of Everything," the architect of our wartime industrialization and the postwar boom. Howe's wilful, bulldog determination and arrogance had made the boom possible, but his "What's a million?" attitude soon would sink him and

---

Previous page: After her successful crossing of Lake Ontario, Marilyn Bell became Canada's sweetheart. Toronto threw a ticker tape parade in her honour in the spring of 1955. Marilyn Bell later went on to become the youngest person to swim the English Channel and B.C.'s Straits of Juan de Fuca.

the St. Laurent government in the wake of the pipeline debate. Before that happened, however, Newfoundland, in a tight vote, would become Canada's tenth province.

Our post-war ideals of saving the world from war, disease, and hunger gradually eroded as we grew rich, fat, and complacent in the solid, stolid years of St. Laurent and Eisenhower. The boom pushed us ever closer to things American in clothes, fads, television, movies, magazines, music, and, most of all, business. Mackenzie King, in one of his last acts before relinquishing the prime ministership after almost twenty-two years, flirted with the idea of free trade with the United States. Fear of powerful Conservative opposition to it ended the flirtation quickly.

Nonetheless, exports to the United States skyrocketed in the fifties, especially during the Korean War. Our factories began feeding the insatiable American war machine, giving us huge profits, even as we preached against Secretary of State John Foster Dulles's "Brink of War" Cold War rhetoric.

Actually, it could be argued that the Cold War started right here in Canada on a sultry early September night in 1945. A Soviet cipher clerk, Igor Gouzenko, stuffed 109 secret documents under his shirt and walked out of the Soviet Embassy in staid old Ottawa into a spy scandal that rocked the world and blasted apart the Big Three's Grand Alliance of the Second World War. His Russian spy-ring revelations staggered Canadians, who quickly and quietly acquiesced in a brutal sweeping aside of civil liberties in the search for traitors. One of these was found to be a Member of Parliament, Fred Rose.

We might avert our eyes at home, but they grew wide with outrage as we watched Senator Joseph McCarthy's vicious "Red Hunt" sweep through the United States on the heels of communist spies stealing atomic secrets, the Alger Hiss case, and the Korean War. And though we watched the Americans in chagrin, we looked on in sadness as Britain went bankrupt; those splotches of pink on maps of the world began to shrink as the British Empire faded away. It was clearly the American Decade in an era of power politics. But while the United States became more powerful, it also became less popular. Even with the supremely generous, life-saving Marshall Plan in Europe, a virulent form of anti-Americanism began spreading around the world.

As the fifties sped by, Canada grew bigger and younger. By 1955, the population had increased forty percent since the war and one-third of all those Canadians were under fourteen. The baby bonus had come in after the end of the war, followed by better old age pensions, housing subsidies, and health insurance. By 1957 the Canada Council was established. While all this was happening, Pierre Trudeau was an obscure professor and writer on the Montreal magazine *Cité Libre* and René Lévesque was Quebec's most popular television commentator.

Our jitterbugging and jiving waned as the years rolled on and we began to dance cheek-to-cheek to the big bands. Suddenly, a decade after the war's end, our music changed. Jukeboxes blasted our eardrums; Bill Haley and his Comets were raucously signalling the start of a new rock 'n' roll era with "Rock Around the Clock."

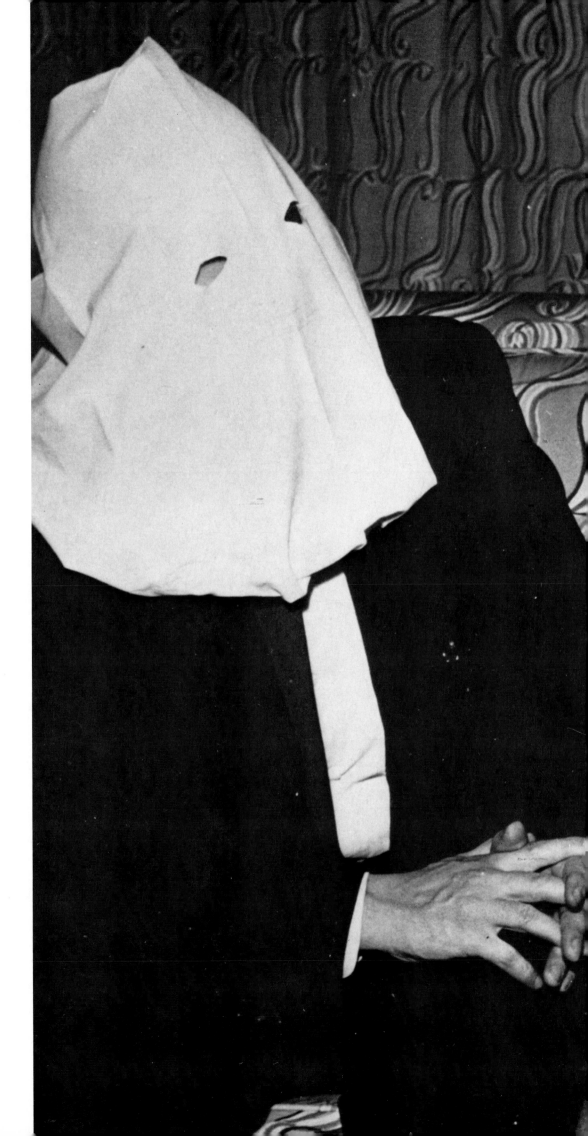

Left: Barbara Ann Scott, every young girl's dream in the late 1940s, executes the "Stag Jump" that was a hallmark of her style. In the 1948 St. Moritz Olympics she won the gold medal for figure skating and was named Canada's athlete of the year in 1945, 1947, and 1948.

Right: Igor Gouzenko at the time of the publication of his novel *The Fall of a Titan* in 1954. Gouzenko was a Russian cipher clerk in Ottawa who defected in 1945. His allegations that there were major Soviet espionage networks operating in Canada led to many arrests and a Royal Commission investigation. Gouzenko and his family were given new identities and spent the rest of their lives under police protection. Whenever he appeared in public, it was always in the mask he wears in this photograph.

Left: Evelyn Dick, the focus of two sensational murder trials, leaves the Hamilton Courthouse in 1947. She was found not guilty of the murder of her husband, John Dick, whose torso, without arms, legs, or head, had been found on the Hamilton Escarpment. Another jury, however, convicted her of manslaughter when the body of her infant son was found entombed in cement in an attic bedroom.

Right: D. M. Candon of Detroit escapes from the flaming *Noronic* on September 17, 1949, with briefcase in hand and a cigar in his mouth. The *Noronic* was a steamer of the Canadian Steamship Lines Ltd. that normally sailed between Detroit, Michigan, and Duluth, Minnesota. On a rare trip to Toronto it caught fire at dockside and 118 lives were lost.

Joseph (Joey) Smallwood signs the agreement admitting Newfoundland to Confederation. Newfoundland had originally rejected Confederation in 1867 and sentiment against the move remained high decades later. It took two referenda and an intense campaign by Smallwood for the Confederation side to win even a narrow majority. Newfoundland officially became Canada's tenth province on March 31, 1949.

Right: Toronto Postmaster W. M. MacLean closes the inaugural ceremonies of the Post Office's "all-up" mail service in 1948 by loading the last bag of letters into a North Star's baggage compartment; city controller John Innes looks on. Canada was the first country in the world to introduce domestic service in which first-class mail is carried by air at regular postage rates.

The Grey Cup is one of the biggest and most exciting sports events of the year. Here, in the heyday of the Toronto Argonauts, is the sloppy game of 1950 won by the Argos. It was affectionately dubbed the "Mud Bowl."

Rocket Richard, the most popular member of the Montreal Canadiens hockey team from 1942 to 1960, caught his skate in the glass
while falling at the Maple Leaf Gardens in this famous shot. Richard's
competitiveness and scoring prowess made him the most admired
player of the era.

Left: The funeral procession for former Prime Minister William Lyon Mackenzie King pulls away from Parliament Hill on July 26, 1950. Leader of the Liberal Party from 1919 to 1948, he was prime minister for almost twenty-two of those years and has continued to arouse controversy long after his death. Seen as a rather colourless and even priggish man by many of his contemporaries, he later revealed in his journals a bizarre and secret life.

The young Princess Elizabeth caught in a wonderful, informal moment in October 1951. The occasion was a square dance held at Government House in Ottawa. Two years later, loyal Canadians would travel to England for her coronation or watch a film entitled *A Queen Is Crowned* in their local theatres.

Previous Pages: Bill Barilko of the Toronto Maple Leafs scores the winning goal of the final Stanley Cup hockey game of the 1951 season. One week later, he was killed in a plane crash. The Stanley Cup, the oldest trophy competed for by North American professional athletes, has been associated with professional hockey since 1910.

Above: Volunteer crews and Canadian servicemen fill sandbags as they battle the rising waters of the Red River in the Winnipeg suburb of St. Vital, April 24, 1950. The flood, considered one of the worst in North America, forced 100,000 to flee Winnipeg and left 80,000 homeless.

Left: A young CBC journalist, René Lévesque, interviews a Canadian soldier on the banks of the Imjin River in Korea, August 14, 1951. Canada participated in the Korean War as part of the United Nations' forces.

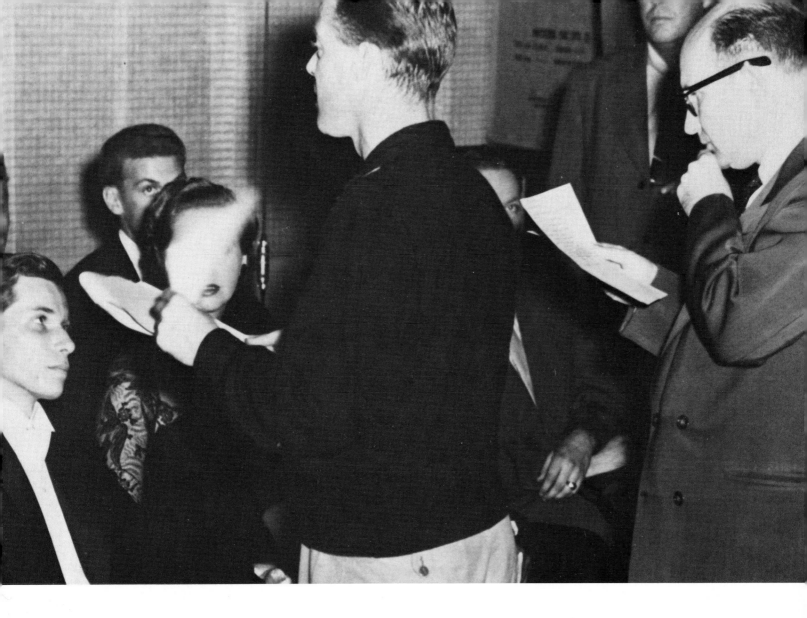

Previous pages: The Boyd Gang in Toronto after their second capture, September 1952. These notorious bank robbers made a daring escape from Toronto's Don Jail on September 8, 1952, precipitating the largest manhunt in Canadian history. Eight days later, they were recaptured after a gun battle at a North York barn. Edwin Boyd (with bowed head), leader of the gang, was paroled in 1966 and now lives in western Canada under an assumed name.

Above: The inaugural broadcast of CBC's first night of regular television programming on September 8, 1952, featured a variety special entitled "Kaleidoscope." In this photograph, producer Drew Crossan *(second from right, foreground)* and Mavor Moore *(extreme right)*, then chief producer, brief the opening night cast which included a relatively unknown twenty-year-old pianist named Glenn Gould, program host John Fisher, singers Terry Dale, Wally Koster, Fran Wright, and Jan Rubes, sportscaster Dave Price and his guest Ted Reeve, and Geoffrey Waddington.

Left: Incorporated in November 1952, the Stratford Festival presented its first three plays the following summer, officially opening with a production of *Richard III* directed by Tyrone Guthrie and starring Alec Guinness. The pillared, thrust stage is a striking feature of the theatre.

In the early 1950s, shopping malls and supermarkets changed the shopping habits of a nation. The mall concept was pioneered in Canada by Bill Zeckendorf, the king of the fifties' developers. This photograph shows the excitement of the opening of one of Toronto's first malls, at Bathurst and Lawrence, on October 31, 1953. People were willing to line up for a chance to investigate the new shopping experience.

Right: Canada's first subway line opened in Toronto on March 30, 1954. Flashing the green light on the Yonge St. line are Ontario Premier Leslie Frost and Toronto Mayor Alan Lamport.

Left: At the age of 16, Marilyn Bell became the first person to swim across Lake Ontario from Youngstown, New York, to Toronto on September 10, 1954. Braving bitter cold and lamprey eels, she made the 52 kilometre crossing in 21 hours. She is seen here being helped into a boat by lifeguards after she touched the Toronto breakwater.

Running history was made at the British Empire Games in Vancouver on August 7, 1952, when Dr. Roger Bannister of England narrowly beat John Landy of Australia, marking the first time two contestants ran the mile in less than four minutes.

Left: Hurricane Hazel ripped through central and southern Ontario in October 1954, dumping over 100 millimetres of rain on the Metropolitan Toronto area in just 12 hours. Eighty-one people died in the worst natural disaster the area would see until the Barrie tornado of 1985.

Lake Erie fishermen rescue the survivors of the *Ciscoe* which ran aground on a sandbar and was battered for five hours by heavy seas on March 24, 1955. One man was drowned in the incident.

Above: "Don Messer's Jubilee," one of the most popular TV shows ever aired on CBC, featured the old-time "down-east" music of Don Messer and his Islanders. Its cancellation in 1969 aroused a storm of protest from die-hard fans, but the CBC decided not to resurrect the program. Don Messer (with fiddle) is shown here with Charlie Chamberlain on guitar and the Islanders band on the opening night of the program on CBC-TV Halifax in 1956.

Above right: Rocket Richard of the Montreal Canadiens was suspended from play for the remainder of the season in March 1955 after he struck Boston Bruin player Hal Laycoe and attacked another Bruin who tried to intervene. Clarence Campbell, president of the National Hockey League, is shown being accosted in the Montreal Forum by an irate fan after the announcement of Richard's suspension. This incident created a brawl that erupted into the streets–the worst sports riot Canada has seen.

Below right: Foster Hewitt, Canada's beloved hockey announcer, dominated radio and later TV NHL coverage for the whole of his long career. He did the first hockey broadcast in 1923, switched to TV in the 1950s and continued to be the "voice of hockey" until his retirement shortly before his death in 1985.

57-66 The Tempestuous Years

It was a "youthquake." Symbolizing the nation's bursting out of the dull conventionality of the Eisenhower and "Uncle Louis" St. Laurent era, the young of Canada rocked to the defiant sexuality of Elvis Presley slapping the guitar dangling at his thumping, pumping hips and groaning "You ain't nuthin' but a hound dog." A few years later, they screamed in ecstatic adoration at the mop-haired Beatles singing "A Hard Day's Night."

Music influenced our lives as never before. Our baby-boomers, now jeans-clad teenagers, flocked to the coffee houses in Vancouver, Calgary, Ottawa, and Toronto's Yorkville, turning on to Gordon Lightfoot, Joni Mitchell, and Neil Young. They burst the crowded classrooms, made Marshall McLuhan their guru, and read the Beat generation poetry of Allen Ginsberg and Jack Kerouac's *On the Road*. Some tuned in, turned on, and dropped out on sex, drugs, and rock 'n' roll; others more innocently O.D.'d on pizzas and hamburgers and whirled a hula hoop.

Credit cards became a status symbol for the spend-now-pay-later, plastic-money generation, and taboos fell before the onslaught of the Pill, relaxed divorce laws, and "free love." We gobbled up steamy, sex-soaked *Peyton Place* and *Lady Chatterley's Lover,* as well as thumbing the pages of *Playboy,* but our interest in Canadian authors, such as Mordecai Richler and Hugh MacLennan, was beginning to grow.

Our polio fears ended with the Salk vaccine, possibly the most important medical breakthrough of the decade. Most of us had cars by now, and we travelled more, belching over the landscape across wide new roads, including the long-awaited Trans-Canada Highway.

On television, we watched "I Love Lucy," "The Plouffe Family," and, after the hockey game on Saturday nights, "Our Pet" Juliette. In shock we saw the Hungarian Revolution and the Suez Canal crisis; and in wonder we saw Sputnik, Yuri Gagarin, and John Glenn.

British Prime Minister Harold Macmillan spoke of "the winds of change" in Africa; he could have applied it to Europe with its new Common Market. The "winds of change" were blowing across Canada, too–the long-reigning Liberal government was sputtering into oblivion. Howling out of the Prairies, jowls jiggling and eyes flashing, came that evangelical populist prophet of "One Canada," John Diefenbaker. He overwhelmed the tired, old St. Laurent Liberals and, with the election of Lester B. Pearson as the new Liberal leader, one of Canada's most tempestuous political eras began. "Dief the Chief" and "Mike" Pearson clashed not only in their political differences but in personal animosity.

Thrashing about in the politics of histrionics, Diefenbaker killed the Avro Arrow, proclaimed his Bill of Rights, fired James Coyne, the governor of the Bank of Canada, fought off continuous real and imagined plots against him by fellow Conservatives. He plunged relations with the president to their lowest level ever. He told friends that John F. Kennedy was a "boastful young son of a bitch," and JFK reciprocated by calling Diefenbaker a liar, a bore and a cheat, especially when Dief ridiculed the Kennedy Bay of Pigs fiasco and later withheld support for the U.S. during the Cuban Missile Crisis.

Previous page: Prime Minister Pearson with President John F. Kennedy at Hyannis Port, Massachusetts in the spring of 1963, shortly after Pearson's election.

But Canadians had fallen in love with the style and youthful exuberance of Kennedy and his New Frontier. We shared his feelings as he cried that "the torch has been passed to a new generation." The Kennedy verve contrasted sharply with the cabinet back-biting and the surly squabbles about Diefenbaker's leadership and the issue of whether Canada had or had not committed itself to accept nuclear arms. Diefenbaker was damaged, too, by the "Diefenbuck," a Liberal gimmick symbolizing the sorry state of the Canadian dollar–now worth a mere 92.5¢ American.

When the Diefenbaker government politically imploded in 1963, Kennedy was delighted, and Pearson, as the new prime minister, quickly repaired relations with the White House. But he, like all of us, was transfixed with horror as Earl Cameron showed us the televised pictures of Kennedy's assassination in Dallas. We tried to adjust to the shrewd new president, Lyndon Baines Johnson. Our horror grew as we saw our American neighbours explode into a kind of anarchy with race riots in Selma, Watts, and Birmingham, and with the growing Vietnam disaster.

If there was anarchy in the United States, there was chaos in Canada. We followed the scandals of Hal Banks, Lucien Rivard, and Gerda Munsinger, saw the doctors' strike in Saskatchewan, the bitter debate over a new Canadian flag, and unification of the armed forces. Throughout all of it, the Quiet Revolution in Quebec was becoming increasingly less quiet.

Mike Pearson's polka-dot bow tie and cherubic smile seemed to wilt under the onslaught. But in the end, he–and we–got the flag, the armed forces were unified, and medicare, the Canada Pension Plan, and the auto pact with the United States all came about. And we also got ready for our 1967 Centennial celebrations and Montreal's Expo 67: the biggest, most successful party in the history of the nation.

Elvis Presley, rock'n'roll idol of the 1950s, toured Canada briefly in 1957. Born in Mississippi and reared on gospel music, Elvis was one of the first white singers to popularize black rhythm-and-blues music for a mainstream middle-America audience. Canadian teenagers went wild over his music and rumour had it that the dust from the stages where he appeared was swept up and sold after his performances.

William Shatner and Corinne Connelly in a CBC "kitchen-sink" drama of the late 1950s. William Shatner went on to fame and fortune as Captain Kirk in the immensely popular American television series "Star Trek."

Louis St. Laurent at the end of his political career in the late 1950s.
St. Laurent was prime minister from 1948 to 1957, presiding over the
greatest period of economic growth and prosperity Canada has
ever seen.

Centre: The famous Avro Arrow interceptor jet is seen here at its first public display in 1957. Hailed by Canadians as the most technologically advanced fighter of its time, its production was cancelled by the Diefenbaker government in 1959 on the grounds that costs were too high and that bomber threats could be met more effectively with missiles. The cancellation caused much public outcry and is considered by some to have sounded the death-knell for Canada's independent aircraft industry.

Lester B. (Mike) Pearson and Mrs. Pearson in Oslo, Norway, where Pearson was awarded the Nobel Peace Prize in 1957 for his role in creating a United Nations peacekeeping force during the Suez Crisis of November 1956. The peacekeeping forces, composed of ser-vicemen from a number of different countries, are still active and effective today in policing the trouble spots of the world. Pearson was one of Canada's best-loved politicians. Serving originally in the diplomatic service, he entered politics in 1948, was leader of the opposition from 1958 until the Liberal victory of 1963, and prime minister until his retirement in 1968.

Weary and blackened with coal dust, rescue worker John Totten (*left*) tells his brother William of progress in the search for victims of the coal mine disaster in Springhill, Nova Scotia. A tunnel in the mine collapsed on October 23, 1958, trapping 93 men 3,960 metres below the ground. Seventeen of the trapped men were rescued–the deepest rescues executed in Canada. William Totten, one of the rescued men, returned to help.

Right: Canada's record for accepting refugees during the 1930s and the war years was appalling. By the 1950s, however, a booming economy, a need for manpower, and a growing awareness of the outside world brought about a more open attitude toward immigration. When the Hungarian uprising against the Soviets was crushed in 1956, Canada welcomed nearly 38,000 refugees. Here a father and a son disembark in their new country in 1957.

Left: President Dwight Eisenhower points out features of the St Lawrence Seaway to Queen Elizabeth II as they sail along it aboard the Royal Yacht *Britannia* after the official opening ceremonies of the waterway in 1959. Constructed as a joint project of the Canadian and American governments, the seaway is a series of locks and canals that opens the waters to navigation from Montreal to the Lake Superior lakehead from late winter to mid-December each year.

Above: Pomp and ostentation marked Maurice Duplessis's funeral in September 1959. Known as *"le Chef"* during his long and colourful career, Duplessis ruled Quebec with a strong and autocratic arm, keeping the province isolated and conservative. With his passing, the liberal, progressive element of Quebec society could finally gain some ground, bringing in the Quiet Revolution of the 1960s under Premier Jean Lesage.

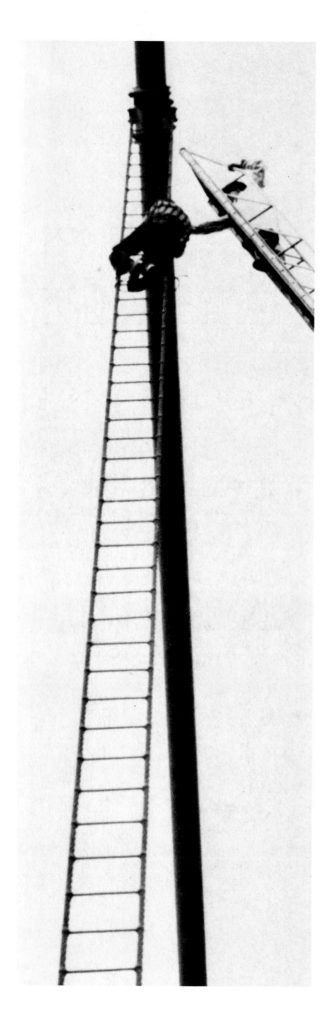

Left: Vancouver fireman Len Erlandson executes a daring rescue of a would-be suicide 300 feet above the water on the Lions Gate Bridge. The man, on the verge of fainting as Erlandson reached him, nonetheless fought attempts to rescue him for 50 minutes.

The 1959 strike of the International Woodworkers of America at the Anglo-Newfoundland Development Company's Grand Falls sawmill was one of the most bitter in Newfoundland's history. The strikers were charged with intimidation tactics by the company, precipitating a riot in which an RCMP officer was killed. Here, some of the 1,200 men on strike are delivered to jail following their arrest.

A backstage photograph of teenage heartthrob singer Paul Anka, who wowed teen fans at a concert session at Maple Leaf Gardens in Toronto in 1959. Rocketing to fame at the age of 15 with his hit song "Diana," Anka was one of the few Canadian pop singers to gain success on both sides of the border in the 1950s.

Right: College campuses of the early 1960s were prone to fads and silliness of the highest order. This 1961 photo shows students from Ryerson Institute of Technology in Toronto attempting to set a record for piling the most people onto a toilet bowl-13. Other popular fads were bed-pushing contests, goldfish-swallowing, and the inevitable beer-drinking competitions.

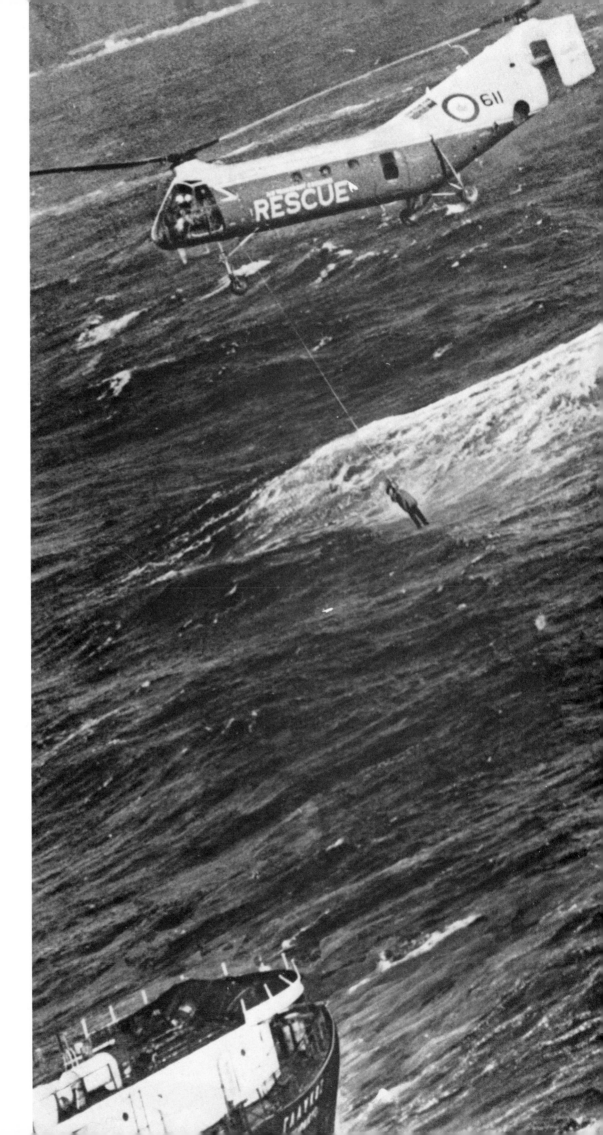

Left: A Doukhobor woman watches as a greenhouse goes up in flames in a protest over compulsory education in British Columbia in 1962. Doukhobors believe in pacifism and simple, communal living and their radical members-called The Sons of Freedom-have opposed compulsory education. In the fifties and sixties, the Sons of Freedom raised a furor by holding nude protests and by burning buildings, often their own, in protest against government intervention in their lives. This belief, in particular, has brought them into conflict with provincial governments on the issue of compulsory education.

Right: An RCAF helicopter rescues a crew member from a grounded Russian freighter off the west coast of Vancouver Island, January 1962.

Above left: Quarterback Jackie Parker of the Edmonton Eskimos catches the football as two Calgary Stampeders close in at a Western Football Conference Game in Calgary in 1962. In 1978, Parker's illustrious sports career was recognized when he was voted the most outstanding player in the Canadian Football League in 25 years. He was awarded the Jeff Nicklin Most Valuable Player Trophy seven times, and the Schenley Outstanding Player Trophy three times.

Below left: "Front Page Challenge," the longest-running show on CBC television, began as a summer replacement in 1957 and is still being aired. Here are the regular and youthful panelists in 1960 sitting in front of a mystery guest. Left to right: Gordon Sinclair, Toby Robins, and Pierre Berton.

Right: "Our Pet, Juliette" was a national byword in the 1950s and 1960s. Juliette hosted an immensely popular television series named after herself immediately following the Saturday night hockey game on CBC-TV from 1956 to 1966. The cancellation of "The Juliette Show" caused a national outcry.

Left: Hula hoops took North America by storm in the late fifties and early sixties. This little champ handles four at once, an amazing feat of co-ordination.

Canada's most famous racing thoroughbred, Northern Dancer, in the winner's circle of the Kentucky Derby in 1964. Owned by E.P. Taylor's Windfield Farms, Northern Dancer was the first Canadian horse to win the Derby. He went on to win the Preakness and, although he lost the Belmont Stakes, he did win the Queen's Plate. He was immediately retired to stud and has since become the world's leading sire.

Above: Harold C. (Hal) Banks, the notorious head of the Canadian branch of the Seafarers' International Union, in 1963. Banks was invited by shipping company interests, in conjunction with the federal government and some elements of the labour movement, to come to Canada in 1949 to drive the Communist-dominated Canadian Seamen's Union out of the Great Lakes. Within two years, he had broken the union and the SIU controlled most of the organized sailors in Canada. It surfaced later, however, that he had used violence and terrorism to gain control. Sentenced to five years in jail in 1964, he fled to the United States while on bail and was never extradited.

Right: A West Coast Airlines plane crashed in a wheatfield just short of the Calgary runway on the night of August 24, 1963. Parts of the tail and undercarriage lie in the trail left by the plane's landing. All 15 passengers aboard survived.

Below: Canada's age of innocence came abruptly to an end with the gathering violence in Quebec. In this chilling photograph, army engineer Sergeant-Major Walter Leja lies gravely wounded in a gutter after attempting to defuse a bomb placed in a mailbox by separatist terrorists in May 1963. Stunned police detectives look on, paralyzed with horror.

Left: Prime Minister John Diefenbaker crosses his fingers while entering the House of Commons on February 5, 1963 to face the non-confidence vote that would bring down his Progressive Conservative government.

Patrick Watson and Laurier LaPierre on the set of CBC's public affairs program "This Hour Has Seven Days." It aired from 1964 to 1966, using "hot seat" interviews and the techniques of investigative journalism. Many of the items first raised on "Seven Days" became major national issues in the press and Parliament but the program attracted controversy and was eventually cancelled.

Canada was hit by Beatlemania as much as any other country. Here, the "fabulous four" arrive for a brief tour in 1964. Screaming fans were often uncontrollable and the police were kept busy.

The Flag Debate of 1964 opened in the House of Commons on June 15 and continued with passion until December 15. The Liberal government originally favoured a flag with three maple leaves. The Progressive Conservatives were violently opposed to any change, favouring the existing Red Ensign which connoted for them continuity and respect for Canada's past. A committee appointed by Prime Minister Pearson eventually came up with the recommendation that resulted in our present flag. Debate did not stop until closure was imposed. Here, Liberal members hold up the new flag, cheer, and sing "O Canada" after the successful vote.

Canadian heavyweight boxer George Chuvalo takes a right from world heavyweight champion Cassius Clay (Muhammad Ali) in the third round of their Toronto bout on March 29, 1966. Although he never won the world championship, Chuvalo outslugged Floyd Patterson and went 15 rounds with Ali.

Gerda Munsinger, a Montreal divorcée originally from East Germany, was the centre of the most sensational sex scandal in Canada, and newspapers eagerly printed this obviously posed picture of her. On December 7, 1960, the RCMP informed Minister of Justice E. Davie Fulton and Prime Minister Diefenbaker that Mrs. Munsinger was having an affair with the Associate Minister of National Defence Pierre Sévigny, and that they considered her a security risk. The matter slipped into oblivion until 1966 when a Liberal minister brought it up during a heated debate in the House of Commons. The subsequent scandal precipitated an inquiry which found some element of a ''security risk'' and stated that Diefenbaker had erred in not demanding the resignation of Sévigny.

John Diefenbaker, then leader of the opposition, addresses the National Progressive Conservative Association meeting in November 1966, when the party voted to hold the leadership review that would send "the Chief" to his defeat. Dalton Camp, who called for the review, is second from right, beside Robert Stanfield, Premier of Nova Scotia, who would become the next leader of the Conservative Party.

67-76
The Pride and Protest Years

Who could ever forget that bursting pride . . . that leaping joy at being a Canadian that suffused us as we celebrated our one hundredth birthday? At Expo 67 we threw a huge, triumphant celebration, symbolized by the tootling horn of Bobby Gimby as a hundred kids skipped along behind his flying cape singing-shouting "CA-NA-DA."

There were twenty million of us now, and a poll showed that 85 percent of us thought Canada was the best country in the world. Then, in our quite un-Canadian euphoria, we suddenly were seized with "Trudeaumania." Here was a man of grace and wit and brains, filled with eloquence and new ideas, sparkling with sexual magnetism and Gallic charm. Enthusiastically, we propelled him into the prime minister's office.

Our love affair with Canada climaxed in 1972 with a universal shriek of exultation when, with thirty-four seconds to go in the final game, Paul Henderson slapped home the winning goal in Moscow to give Team Canada victory over the Russians.

At the same time, there was the reality of the FLQ and the struggle for an independent Quebec. We plunged into the hell-hole of terrorism; never again would we be able to say "but it can't happen here." In October 1970, the FLQ kidnapped British diplomat James Cross and Quebec cabinet minister Pierre Laporte was found murdered; the nation waited tensely until Cross was found and his release negotiated, his captors being allowed to leave Canada for Cuba. The Just Society had turned into the War Measures Act. Trudeau muttered about the "bleeding hearts" who opposed him, and warned them, "Just watch me!" Most of us supported him, but began to wonder–increasingly as time went on–about his cold arrogance and combative disdain.

But our fascination with him was endless. Our bachelor prime minister cavorted with beautiful women, slid down banisters, dressed outrageously. Finally he married Margaret Sinclair, a quarter-century his junior, a Vancouver flower child he'd met while holidaying in Tahiti. It was the romance of the decade to Canadians, not known for their romantic natures. He "taught me all I know about love," said Margaret.

"French power" took over in Ottawa: Marc Lalonde, Jean Marchand, and Gérard Pelletier held the reins and bilingualism became the law. Unilingual English Canadians, especially in the west, fretted about "French on corn flakes boxes" and on their road signs. Quebeckers, powered by a new sense of urgent, hungry pride and stimulated by the upheaval of General de Gaulle's 1967 state visit to the province, when he had shouted, *"Vive le Québec libre,"* spurned the decaying Bourassa Liberals and elected the charismatic, one-time television journalist René Lévesque and his separatist Parti Québécois in 1976. That set the stage for what would be the most dramatic federal-provincial confrontation of the century.

But Canada's internal rumblings were a sidebar to world events. There was the American tragedy in Vietnam and the domestic disarray it caused, spawning such horrors as the Kent State University killings. There were the "Burn, Baby, Burn" race riots; the assassinations of Martin Luther King and Bobby Kennedy; Jerry Rubin and Abby Hoffman and the Weathermen; and, of

Previous page: The visit of de Gaulle spawned a series of demonstrations in Quebec. Here, at a demonstration in Montreal, are prominently displayed the Quebec flag and an RIN *(Rassemblement pour l'indépendance nationale du Québec)* placard. The RIN was a centre-left group of separatists that first ran for election in 1966. They were eventually absorbed into the Parti Québécois.

course, Nixon's Watergate. And there were the continuing Middle East wars and the Russian rape of Czechoslovakia.

But always, our attention returned home. The baby boomers were beginning to have babies of their own, bringing them up on television programs such as "Sesame Street" and "Mr. Dress Up," and moving from the suburbs of the fifties back into the cities. An army of "white painters," they fixed up inner-city slums, ate yogurt and crunchy granola, wore Earth Shoes, jogged, read *The Joy of Sex* cover-to-cover, and talked endlessly about their "relationships." Unmarried couples, homosexuals, and lesbians came "out of the closet." The mini skirt, string bikinis, bra-burning, long hair on everybody, the Woodstock festival, and *Playboy*'s move to full-frontal nudity excited the young, shocked the old, and highlighted this new age of permissiveness.

"The times they are a-changin'," Bob Dylan sang. And as they changed, students tossed frisbees, talked of "flower power," urged each other to "make love not war," welcomed American draft-dodgers into their midst, and marched in protest against almost everything. The hit song "Let the Sun Shine In" was a benign version of Mao's "Let one hundred flowers blossom."

For many die-hard Canadians, however, the worst blow was the 1967 expansion of the NHL from six to twelve teams, giving new meaning to the word *dilution*. Hockey has never been the same since.

Television ruled our roosts. We sat staring at the screen an average of twenty-three hours a week, increasingly finding our heroes, role models, social values, desired lifestyle, and knowledge of the world in that mesmerizing box of wires and tubes. We saw Neil Armstrong walk on the moon and within a few years our awe turned to acceptance as space travel became just another televised event, the astronauts becoming lesser heroes than Guy Lafleur, Bobby Orr, or Ken Dryden. The law required more Canadian content in the programming now, though, so we chuckled with the "King of Kensington," Al Waxman, were informed on world events by Adrienne Clarkson, and hummed along with Anne Murray as she sang barefoot.

In our few hours away from the box, we read Peter Newman's popularized politics and Pierre Berton's popularized histories. The decade that had begun with our self-adulation was drawing to a close with our self-analysis, and this would lead us into a decade of national readjustment.

French President Charles de Gaulle making his famous *"Vive le Québec libre!"* speech in Montreal during the 1967 Centennial celebrations. Prime Minister Pearson took the unprecedented step of publicly rebuking a visiting head-of-state and de Gaulle promptly returned to France.

Right: Queen Elizabeth II is dwarfed by a huge birthday cake in front of the Parliament Buildings in Ottawa, 1967. The Queen, who on July 1 cut the cake to the cheers of thousands of youngsters, was chief among the many heads-of-state who visited Canada during the Centennial year.

Left: John Diefenbaker's wife, Olive, looks over his shoulder as he tallies the results of balloting at the Progressive Conservative convention of 1967 that forced him out of the party leadership. He finally admitted defeat and withdrew after the third ballot.

Pierre Elliott Trudeau acknowledges the cheers of his supporters at the Liberal convention of 1968 at which he won the leadership of the Liberal Party. Trudeau was to change the face of Canadian politics and would dominate the country and his party until his retirement in 1984.

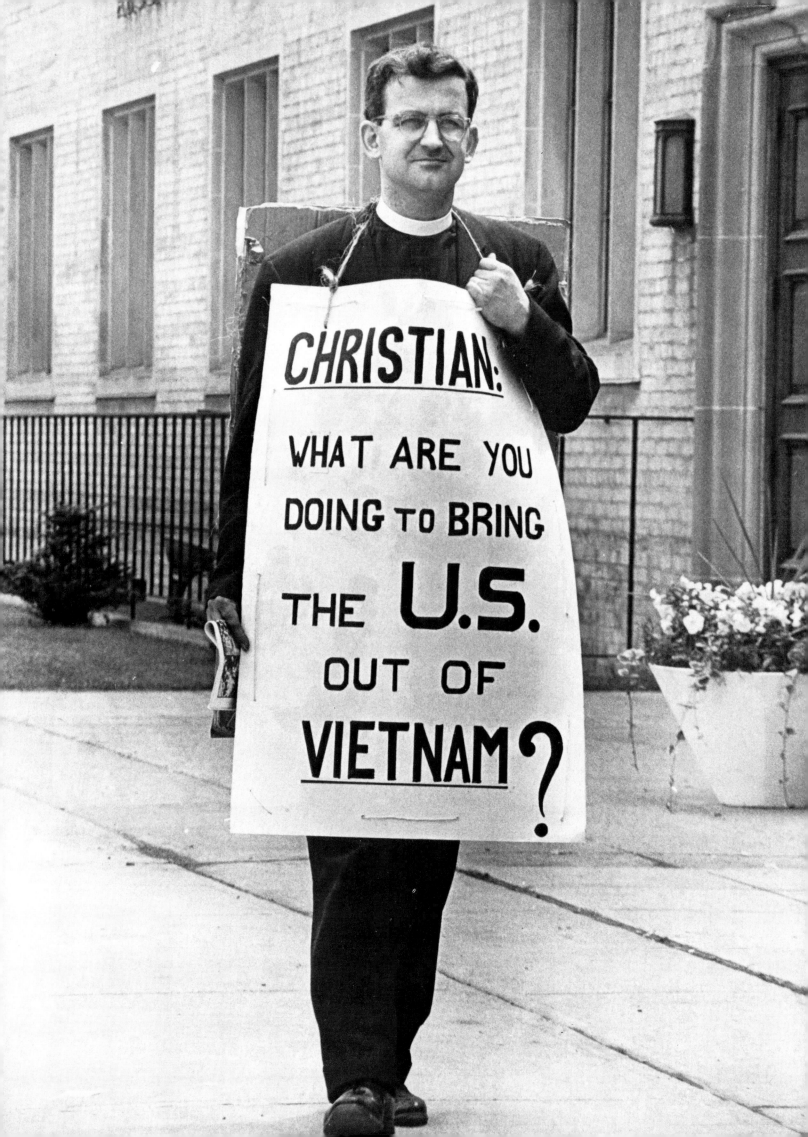

Left: Reverend Dan Heap conducted his one-man protest against the Vietnam War outside the Anglican Diocesan House in Toronto in June 1967. The protest against American participation in Vietnam spilled over into Canada, partly because of the army deserters and draft dodgers who slipped across the border. Most of the draft dodgers who settled in Canada have remained and many have become Canadian citizens.

The sit-in, a common scene in the politically active late 1960s. Here a crowd attends a meeting at Toronto's Queen's Park following a sit-in at City Hall on August 22, 1967. Reverend Durkim, a Methodist pastor from the United States, addresses David DePoe (*standing at right*), a Toronto hippie activist.

Left: The Mary Quant/Carnaby
Street fashion look of 1968.

Right: Former Beatle John Lennon
his wife Yoko Ono travelled to
Toronto in 1968 for a "lie-in" to
"give peace a chance." Later on
this tour, they shocked and titil-
lated the world by posing in the
nude on their hotel bed for
photographers.

Left: A popular phenomenon of the late 1960s was "Miles for Millions" fund raising walks. They were held in towns and cities across the country to raise money for anything from UNICEF to civic buildings.

Right: Nancy Greene, Canada's ski celebrity, speeds down the slalom course at Grenoble, France to win one of the gold medals of the '68 Olympics. In 1967, she had become the World Cup Women's downhill ski champion. In 1968, she won the gold and silver medals for the giant slalom and slalom races in the Grenoble Olympics and a second World Cup. She retired in 1969.

Not all was political unrest and upheaval as the new decade got underway. In this famous picture, a policeman stops four lanes of traffic to let a proud mother duck and her brood cross a rush-hour expressway.

The 1960s' penchant for demonstrations and sit-ins left a lasting legacy–an awareness on the part of the public that lobbying and protest could influence political decisions. In this 1970 picture, citizens of Toronto protest the building of the proposed Spadina Expressway.

A national crisis erupted on October 5, 1970, when the separatist-terrorist FLQ *(Front de libération du Québec)* kidnapped British Trade Commissioner James Cross. A picture of a haggard Cross playing solitaire *(below left)* was released by the terrorists to verify that their prisoner was still alive. On October 10, the same day that the Quebec Department of Justice responded to the FLQ demands and promised safe passage abroad for the kidnappers in return for Cross's release, a second FLQ cell kidnapped the province's Minister of Labour, Pierre Laporte. On October 17, the body of Pierre Laporte was found in the trunk of a car. *(above)* In December, police finally located the cell holding James Cross and negotiated his safe release.

Right: In late December of 1970, the cell of the FLQ responsible for the kidnapping and killing of Pierre Laporte was discovered in Montreal. Its members were arrested and tried in early 1971. Here, an unrepentant Paul Rose, leader of the cell, is shown arriving at court on January 7, 1971. He was found guilty and sentenced to life imprisonment by a Quebec Court of Queen's Bench jury in March 1971, but was granted full parole in December 1982.

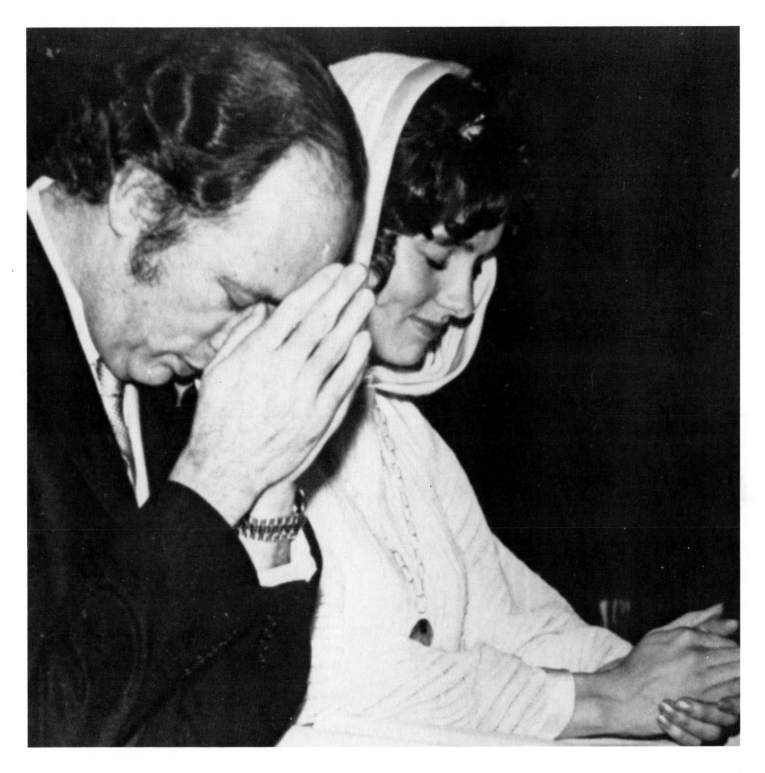

Left: Prime Minister Pierre Trudeau in all his swashbuckling finery at the height of Trudeaumania descends the steps of the Calgary Stadium to kick off the Grey Cup. Canadians initially were bowled over by the novelty of having a sophisticated intellectual as prime minister, and the enthusiasm boiled over into the kind of hysteria usually reserved for rock stars.

The aura of mystery and romance that so infected Canadians in the early Trudeau years was confirmed by the announcement of the secret marriage of Pierre Trudeau to Margaret Sinclair in 1971. Their tempestuous marriage lasted until 1977. They were finally divorced in 1984, with Trudeau retaining custody of their three sons.

Left: The sixties were over, but hippiedom still reigned on the west coast. A typical, freedom-loving family wades on Vancouver's famous nudist Wreck Beach in 1971.

Right: The gay liberation movement was active in the early 1970s, demanding equal rights for homosexuals and attempting to overcome society's prejudices against them. This demonstration took place in the rain on the steps of the Parliament Buildings on August 24, 1971.

Bobby Orr of the Boston Bruins flies through the air after scoring the winning goal in the overtime, sudden-death period of the Stanley Cup finals of 1970. Orr revolutionized the role of the defenceman and is the only defence player to have won the Art Ross Trophy for leading scorer. He was voted Boston's most valuable athlete in history and was, until Wayne Gretzky, the most honoured player in National Hockey League history.

Right: The entire country was on its feet as a cheering Paul Henderson was hugged by Yvon Cournoyer after Henderson had scored the winning goal of the final game of the 1972 Russia-Canada hockey series, with 34 seconds of play remaining. This series was the first to pit the best of Canada's hockey professionals against the famed Soviet team.

Alberta's new Premier, Peter Lougheed, descends the steps of the Legislature flanked by his cabinet in September 1971, after having won the election that threw the Social Credit Party out of power for the first time in 36 years. Using oil resources as a bargaining tool, Lougheed carved out a powerful role for Alberta in Confederation and changed forever the way the rest of Canada looked at the west. He remained undefeated until his retirement in 1985.

Firemen battle a blaze at the Bluebird Café in downtown Montreal on
September 1, 1972. Three men had thrown a firebomb into the lobby
of the nightclub after being refused admittance. Twenty-two people
died in the blaze. At right, an injured man is carried from the building.

A large number of native Indians, mostly women, stream into the Supreme Court in Ottawa on February 22, 1973, for the beginning of an appeal on the status of Indian women married to white men. The case centred on Jeannette Lavell, an Ojibway who had lost her treaty rights when she married a non-Indian. Indian men do not lose their status when they marry non-Indians; in fact, they gain it for their wives and children. Mrs. Lavell argued that this treatment was discriminatory, and contravened the Bill of Rights. In the end, a split court ruled against her appeal.

Right: W. A. C. Bennett, former Social Credit premier of British Columbia, joins the 2,000 people who arrived in Victoria on March 16, 1973, to protest the NDP government's proposed land control legislation. Shortly after this picture was taken, Bennett resigned his seat, lobbying heavily in favour of the election of his son Bill in his place. The NDP never did attempt to pass Bill 42.

Left: This photograph haunted Conservative leader Robert Stanfield throughout the federal election campaign of 1974. In spite of his press image as a dull and unimaginative leader, Stanfield was, in fact, a highly intelligent, compassionate politician who tried to build the Conservative Party into a truly national one that would include representation from Quebec.

Right: Angry Quebec farmers throw milk at Minister of Agriculture Eugene Whelan in Ottawa in 1976 during a demonstration protesting the government's refusal to provide a subsidy for milk.

Left: Marshall McLuhan revolutionized the social science world with his studies on the effects of mass media on thought and behaviour. He insisted that the form in which information is disseminated affects the way in which knowledge is perceived and interpreted.

Canada's musical genius, pianist Glenn Gould, rehearses for a recording session in Toronto in 1974. Gould, a brilliant and eccentric classical musician, was considered to be the world's greatest interpreter of Bach's keyboard music. In 1964 he retired from a successful concert career, preferring recording sessions to the limitations of live performance. In 1982 he died tragically of a stroke, one day after his fiftieth birthday.

Anne Murray shares a joke with Oscar Peterson before being presented with the Order of Canada at Government House in Ottawa in 1983. Although international stars, both musicians have chosen to stay in Canada.

Right: Mikhail Baryshnikov, star of the Soviet Kirov Ballet, dances with the National Ballet of Canada in Toronto in August 1974. Baryshnikov defected from the Soviet Union on June 30, 1974 after a Toronto performance during the Soviet ballet company's 1974 North American tour.

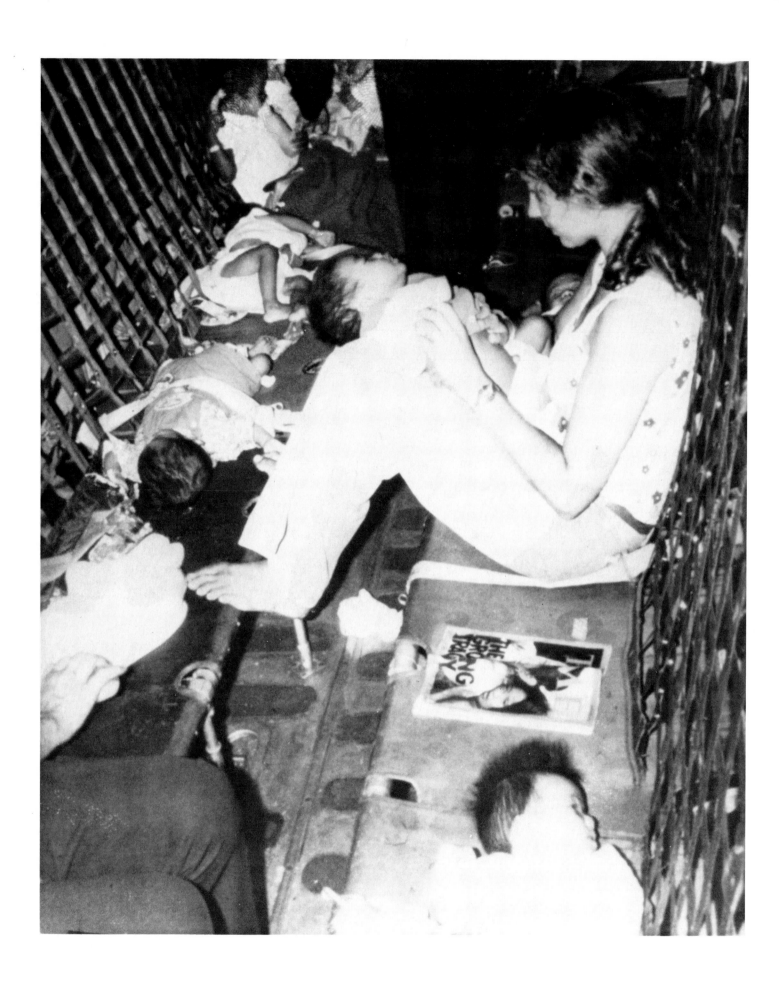

Left: An unidentified woman soothes a Vietnamese baby, one of sixty-two orphans evacuated from South Vietnam by a Canadian Forces aircraft on April 18, 1975, just days before the fall of the Thieu regime. From 1975 to 1981, Canada accepted over 80,000 political refugees from Vietnam.

Right: The final stages in the construction of Toronto's CN Tower, at 553.2 metres (1,815 feet), the tallest free-standing structure in the world. Designed primarily as a telecommunications tower, it has also become a major tourist attraction and Toronto's most prominent landmark.

77-86
The Uncertain Years

Now we had become the "Me Generation."

We were getting cranky, fed up with all the political shouting, the student protests, rising unemployment, wild inflation, and a mean recession. We had grown cynical, acquisitive. Most of all, we were tired of Pierre Trudeau and his thermonuclear temper.

In fact, we were ready to have almost anyone at all in his place. We found Joe Clark, the steadfast, earnest Tory leader, who, with his lost luggage, and a style so utterly different from Trudeau's, dumbfounded even himself by becoming prime minister in September 1979. With a rose in his lapel and a smile on his face, Trudeau told us, "With all its sham, drudgery, and broken dreams, it's still a beautiful world," and, with a wave, drove off in his silver-grey Mercedes convertible.

But by November, bored to tears as opposition leader, Trudeau had quit politics "forever." A month later, the Tories self-destructed in a Parliamentary vote of confidence over their first budget and the cry went out to bring Trudeau back. It worked, and he led the Liberals back to power in as stunning a reversal of political fortunes as Canada had ever seen.

Within weeks he-and all of Canada-focused attention on Quebec and the separatist referendum campaign. René Lévesque was exploiting the pride of Quebeckers to convert Quebec's separate identity into sovereignty-association, in effect, separate nationhood. He almost succeeded. Trudeau stopped him with the greatest speech of his life in Montreal's Paul Sauvé Arena at the end of the campaign, tipping the scales enough to have Quebeckers reject Lévesque's separatism. The issue and its author, Lévesque himself, were on a downward slide ever after.

With that triumph under his belt, Trudeau took on all the premiers in a slam-bang battle about "patriating" the Constitution, and creating a Charter of Rights. The premiers and the entire nation were subjected to his implacable will and icy-eyed rhetoric. In time, he ground everybody down. While he didn't get everything he wanted, he did achieve "patriation" and the Charter, fundamentally changing the nation and guaranteeing himself a significant place in Canadian history.

Trudeau also made history by naming our first socialist governor general, defeated NDP Manitoba Premier Ed Schreyer, and, later, our first woman governor general, Jeanne Sauvé. Her elevation underlined the movement of "Women's Lib" from slogan to reality, with laws and customs changing to accept equality, and women beginning to move into the boardrooms of the nation in book publishing, newspapers, television, labour, business, and education. Flora MacDonald, Maureen McTeer, Shirley Carr, and Supreme Court Justice Bertha Wilson flashed by on our TV screens and newspaper front pages along with the leading members of their international sisterhood, Margaret Thatcher and Indira Gandhi.

We grew more pre-occupied with a healthy economy than with social justice; Lee Iacocca and Conrad Black, the Reichmanns and the Belzbergs became media heroes. The prime concern of university students turned from protest to jobs. Young and old alike were eating health foods, "keeping fit,"

Previous page: Wayne Gretzky, hockey's *wunderkind*, and the Edmonton Oilers carry off the Stanley Cup in 1984. In 1978, at age 17, Gretzky joined the Oilers, becoming the youngest professional playing a major-league sport in North America. He tied for the position of leading scorer in the league in his first season and has since won the Hart Trophy five times, and the Art Ross Trophy four times.

drinking white wine spritzers, and giving up smoking. We seemed to begin every sentence with "Hopefully . . ." and to end every conversation with "Have a nice day!" Hippies had turned into yuppies – young urban professionals – and they were *into* VCRs, microwaves, computers, satellite dishes, BMWs, and T-bills. Others, with their eye on greater concerns, worried about acid rain, pollution, the environment, cruise missiles, and "Star Wars."

Empty nesters whose children had moved out of the suburban bungalows bought downtown condos, sipped in wine bars, nibbled sushi, lasagna, and tofu, listened nostalgically to "The Music of Your Life," and bought lottery tickets from huckstering governments which so recently had frowned on even the sale of Irish Sweepstake tickets.

We didn't hear much talk any longer about the "Just Society" and the government having "no business in the bedrooms of the nation," especially as we watched the unfolding scandals of the RCMP breaking into offices, burning barns, opening mail, and other violations of the law in pursuit of enemies of the state.

A new wave of immigration flowed over the country, this time from the Caribbean, Vietnam, India, Pakistan, Japan, and Hong Kong, but our growing streak of conventionality was more jarred by the sight of punkers with spikes of orange, green, or pink hair, in torn shirts and pants strutting down Yonge Street, Robson Street, or St. Catherines Street; by the omnipresence of the Sony Walkman; by the increasingly loud demonstrations for Gay and Lesbian Rights; and by the turmoil over Dr. Henry Morgentaler's abortion clinics.

We cheered squeaky-clean heroes – Terry Fox on the road, Wayne Gretzky on the ice, and Marc Garneau in space – but on the front pages and on "The National" and "The Journal," we saw President Reagan, half Rambo and half Dale Carnegie, happy in his anecdotal right-wing certainties, struggling to bring about a "Reaganomics" revolution to achieve both more guns and more butter with less taxes and less government.

Over the horizon were wars and terrorism and the papers were filled with strange-sounding names like Khomeini, Arafat, and Khaddafy. The Russians invaded Afghanistan, the Argentinians and then the British invaded the Falklands, the Israelis invaded Lebanon, and the Americans invaded Grenada. Canadian diplomat Ken Taylor was practically canonized for helping the American Embassy diplomats to escape from their captured embassy in Tehran. Ronald Reagan was shot; a month and a half later, so was the Pope. The world seemed to go crazy with shootings, bombings, massacres, hijackings, and air attacks.

Frightened by what we saw overseas and drained by the exhausting, exasperating, if at times exhilarating, roller-coaster years of Trudeau at home, we longed for a quiet corner in which to catch our breath. We yearned for what we nostalgically remembered as the quiet, comfortable, rich times of Eisenhower and St. Laurent.

Pierre Trudeau, too, may have been longing for some peace and quiet. He took his walk in the snow one night and decided to quit politics again, this time for good. The nation heaved a collective sigh of relief. Neither Trudeau's successor, John Turner, nor the Tory leader, Brian Mulroney, had his driven, single-minded, almost contemptuous missionary zeal. We wanted a healing period; Mulroney, percolating with Irish charm in every fibre and back-slapping his way across the country, seemed just the ticket. We gave him the biggest majority in Canadian history and he launched his politics of conciliation.

If browsing through these news photographs of Canada's last half century teaches us anything, it is that we have come of age as a country. The faces in this book, some famous, many unknown, are a reflection of the times we have lived through. In many ways we have changed. In many ways we are the same. The twenty-five million souls living in Canada as 1986 draws to a close might well have a sense of *déjà vu* as we see our prime minister championing free trade with the Americans, rekindling all the old arguments of nationalism that have been with us since we began as a nation nearly 120 years ago.

Left: Prison violence has been escalating over the last decade, as inmates protest conditions in Canada's prisons. Here, inmates Dwight Lowe and Dwight Lucas hold two guards at knifepoint during a hostage-taking in New Westminster, B.C. in February 1976.

Above: An unlikely setting for a government inquiry. Justice Thomas Berger listens to the residents of Nahanni Butte, Northwest Territories, during the Mackenzie Valley Pipeline hearings. Justice Berger took the unprecedented step of taking his inquiry to the people affected by it, instead of insisting that they come to him in an urban centre.

Above: This was the scene on July 17, 1976, in Montreal as athletes and dancers packed the Olympic Stadium during the opening ceremonies of the Summer Olympic Games. The Montreal Olympics marked the first time a Canadian city had hosted the Games, but the controversy over the cost over-runs of the games and its stadium continues to haunt its memory.

Above right: Greg Joy of Vancouver competes for the gold medal in high jumping at the 1976 Montreal Olympics. During this jump, he hit the bar with his foot, losing his chance at the gold. His efforts won the silver medal for Canada.

Below right: Toronto swimmer Cindy Nicholas is greased before plunging into the English Channel to set a new women's record for swimming the Channel, July 18, 1975. In 1977, Nicholas also became the first woman to complete a double crossing.

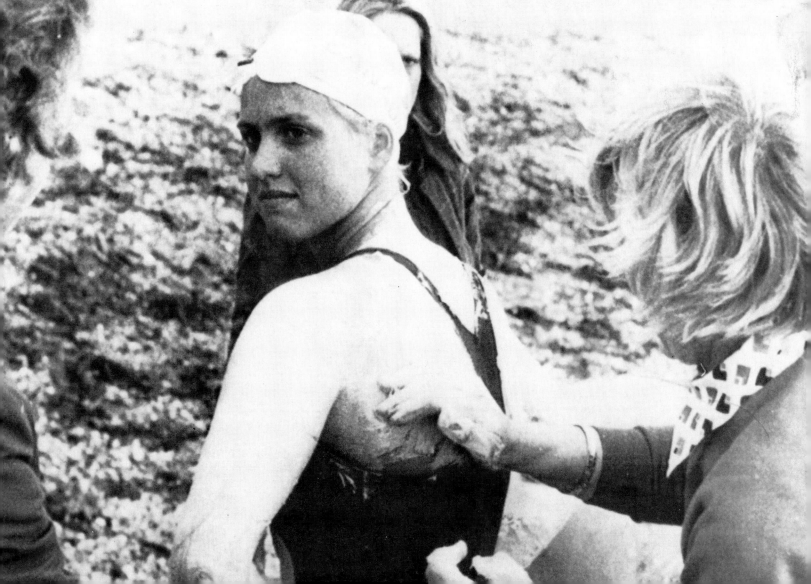

Above left: Prime Minister Pierre Elliott Trudeau loved the outrageous and unexpected public gesture. In this famous photograph, he pirouettes behind Her Majesty Queen Elizabeth II at a Buckingham Palace reception for Commonwealth heads-of-state in 1977.

Above: Guy Lafleur, a much-loved hockey player for the Montreal Canadiens, shoots the puck past the St. Louis Blues' goalie to set a record of 23 consecutive point scoring games on March 24, 1974. He was almost as famous for his refusal to wear a helmet on the ice as he was for his goal-scoring prowess. On December 20, 1983, he became only the tenth player in the history of the National Hockey League to score 500 goals.

Below left: Shortly after being among the first authors to be honoured by the newly formed Canadian Academy of Authors in 1977, Pierre Berton, Farley Mowat, Margaret Laurence, and Leslie McFarlane (*left to right*) attack their celebratory cake with maniacal glee.

Prime Minister-elect Joe Clark and his wife Maureen McTeer on the night of the Conservative federal election victory in May 1979. At the divided Progressive Conservative convention of 1976, Clark had emerged as the "dark horse" winner. His election victory in 1979 made him Canada's youngest-ever prime minister. His government was also one of the shortest-lived, falling victim to a vote of non-confidence in December 1979.

This photograph of John Diefenbaker on holiday in Barbados is one of the last ever taken of "the Chief". He died at Ottawa on August 16, 1979. Defiant and contentious to the end, Diefenbaker held on to his seat in Parliament despite the defeat that toppled him from the leadership of the Conservative Party in 1967. He had been re-elected for the thirteenth time just months before his death.

Three generations of the George Jenzen family watch and wave as
John Diefenbaker's funeral train passes their barley field in
Saskatchewan on August 21, 1979. Diefenbaker had carefully
planned every aspect of his state funeral himself, including the funeral
train and his burial at the Diefenbaker Centre at the University of
Saskatchewan in Saskatoon.

Firemen fight to contain the chemical fire resulting from the train derailment at Mississauga, Ontario, on November 11, 1979. Two hundred thousand people were evacuated from the area.

Right: Firemen remove charred bodies from the reception hall at Chapais, Quebec, on January 1, 1979. Forty-one people died and 40 others were injured when the overcrowded reception hall burst into flames during a New Year's Eve party. A twenty-one-year-old man was later charged with causing the fatal blaze by playing with a lighter around the dried-out evergreen boughs decorating the hall.

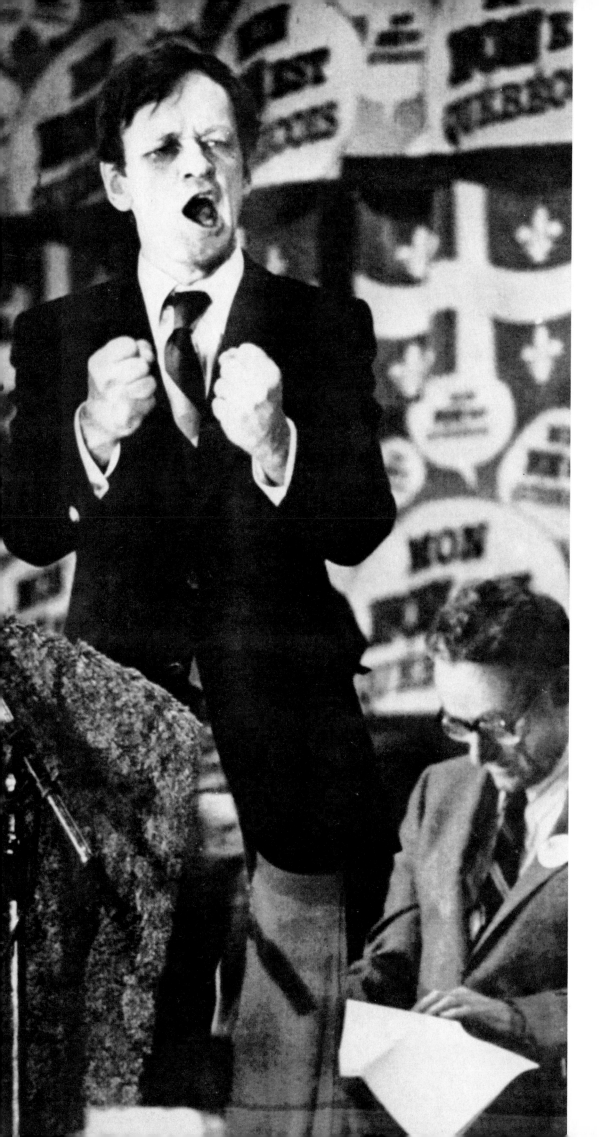

Left: In the months leading up to the referendum in which citizens of Quebec would vote for or against sovereignty-association, Jean Chrétien caught the hearts and minds of Canadians as he passionately fought the issue of Quebec secession. Here Chrétien speaks to a "No" rally in Hull, Quebec, just one month before the vote. Seated at his right is Quebec Liberal leader Claude Ryan.

Above right: Here in Quebec City is a house divided. A "No" committee moved into half the house in April 1980. The residents of the other half retaliated by plastering their half of the house with "Oui" signs.

Below right: Premier René Lévesque fights back tears as he acknowledges the defeat of his party's stand in the referendum. The outcome undermined the very base on which the Parti Québécois was built. Lévesque resigned in 1985 and the Parti Québécois under Pierre-Marc Johnson was defeated later that year.

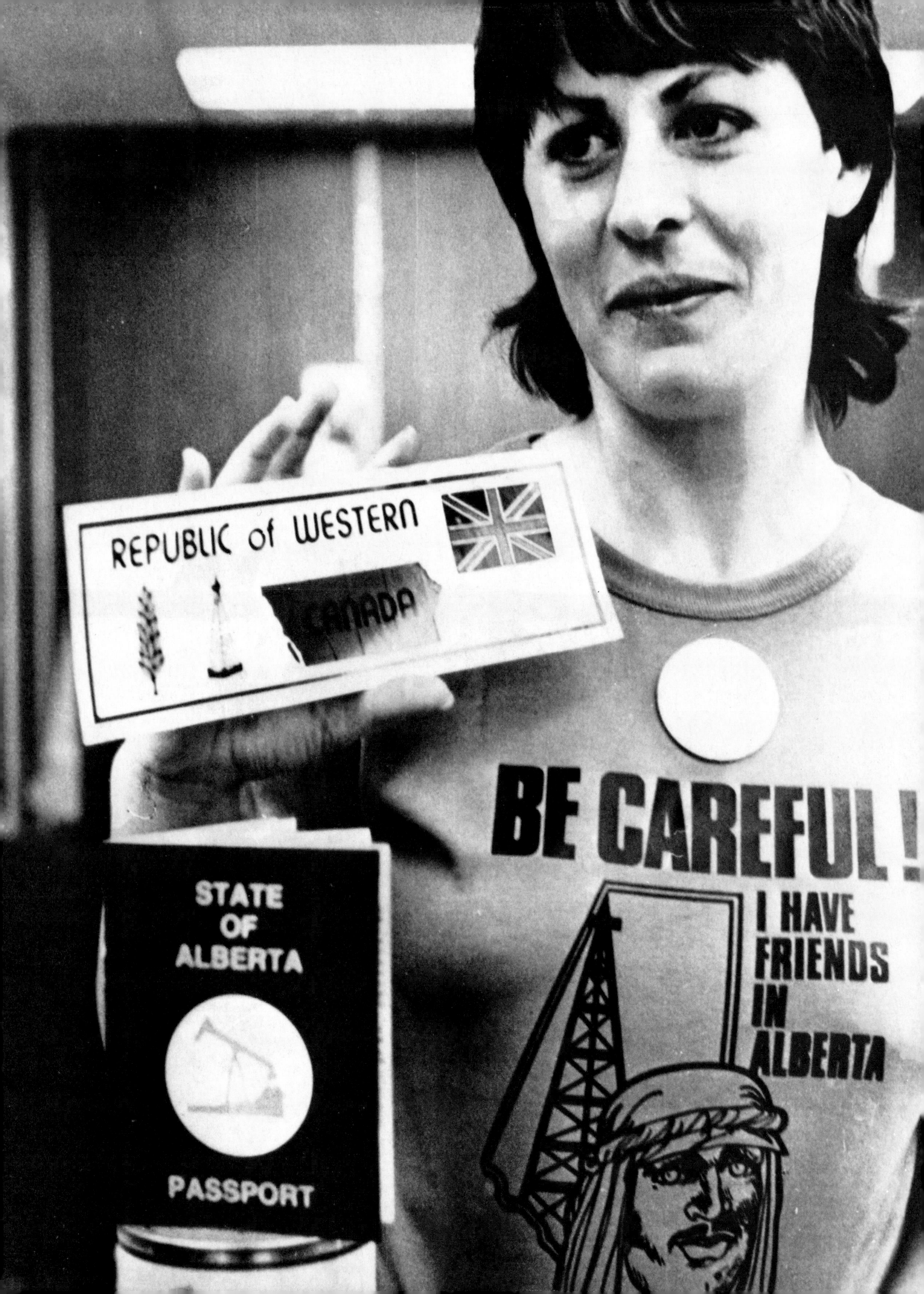
REPUBLIC of WESTERN
CANADA
BE CAREFUL !
I HAVE
FRIENDS
IN
ALBERTA
STATE
OF
ALBERTA
PASSPORT

Left: Quebec is not the only place in Canada where separation raises its head; the western provinces have had periods of serious disaffection as well. This woman displays items that appeared in western stores in 1980, a time when relations between Ottawa and Alberta were particularly strained.

Right: One of the most horrifying murder stories in Canada's history surfaced with the apprehension of Clifford Olson of Port Coquitlam, British Columbia, in 1981. Charged initially with first degree murder of fourteen-year-old Judy Kozma, Olson went on to confess to the sexual assault murders of 11 other children and led police to their burial sites after being promised $100,000 by the RCMP as a reward. When the public learned of this, the arrangement created a widespread reaction of outrage and protest.

Left: Canada Post employees display one of two mailbags received from Los Angeles in February 1980 thanking Canadians for our embassy's efforts in successfully getting American embassy employees out of Tehran during the Iranian hostage crisis. When the American embassy was seized and its employees held hostage by Iranian revolutionaries, Canadian Ambassador Ken Taylor and his staff successfully hid six Americans for over two months and then daringly spirited them out of the country under Canadian passports. Americans responded with jubilant gratitude and Canadians were the heroes of the day.

Prime Minister Pierre Trudeau sits with Queen Elizabeth II at the historic signing of the documents that gave Canada its own constitution. The Constitution Act was proclaimed on April 17, 1982, ending years of wrangling and negotiation between the federal government and the provinces about the content and structure of a new constitution. Canada had been functioning under the British North America Act of 1867, an act of the British Parliament.

Left: Terry Fox, the one-legged cancer victim who won the hearts of Canadians with his "Marathon of Hope," a courageous attempt at a cross-country run to raise funds for cancer research, travels across southern Ontario on an early morning in July 1980. He began his run in St. John's, Newfoundland, on April 12, 1980, but was forced to cancel it at Thunder Bay, when it was discovered that cancer had entered his lungs. He died on June 28, 1981.

Right: Greenpeace crew member Jos Van Hauman, at right, is arrested in 1982 by an RCMP officer as he illegally dyes a harp seal pup on the ice at the annual Gulf of St Lawrence seal hunt. The seal hunt has been a controversial and emotional issue over the last decade: animal conservationists have tried with a fair amount of success to disrupt the hunt and the sale of seal fur. This has adversely affected local hunters, primarily Newfoundlanders, who depend upon the hunt for a substantial portion of their annual income.

Left: Demonstrations and marches have become a Vancouver way of life. In 1983, over 65,000 people marched in an almost festive atmosphere to protest the arms race.

Above right: The British Columbia peace march of 1983 may have looked like a holiday outing, but the Solidarity protest marches later that year were deadly serious. As newly re-elected Premier Bill Bennett began to implement his restraint program, an unprecedented cross-section of labour, civil rights groups, and ordinary people formed the Solidarity Coalition to protest the government's actions. In July, August, and October, mammoth protest marches (the largest with over 50,000 people) took place in Vancouver. It was the greatest grass-roots civil protest Canada has ever seen.

Below right: Canada's agreement with the United States to permit testing of cruise missiles over Canadian territory raised a storm of protest across the country. Anti-cruise protester Dave Savage camped out on Parliament Hill in November 1983 in an attempt to alter government opinion on the issue. Despite the snow and cold temperatures, Savage and others continued their "Peace Camp" vigil.

Left: A pat on Liberal Party President Iona Campagnolo's derrière damaged Liberal leader John Turner's 1984 election campaign, particularly after Turner defended his practice as "friendly." Chris Bauman of Kitchener, Ontario, models a "Turner Shield," the response of a Kitchener women's group to Turner's unfortunate habit. The green form-fitting cardboard protector sold for $1.

Above right: Brian Mulroney and his wife Mila walk through placard-waving supporters to the podium to address the Progressive Conservative leadership convention in June 1983. Mulroney, who had run for leader unsuccessfully in 1976, won at this convention, even though he had never been an M.P. in the House of Commons.

Below right: New Democratic Party leaders from across Canada take a break from the national NDP convention in Regina on July 1, 1983, to don chef's hats and serve a giant birthday cake to celebrate the fiftieth anniversary of the founding of the Co-operative Commonwealth Federation. *Left to right:* Dave Barrett, British Columbia; Allan Blakeney, Saskatchewan; Grant Notley, Alberta; Alexa McDonough, Nova Scotia; party president Tony Penikett; national leader Ed Broadbent; and Bob Rae, Ontario.

Left: In a sensational murder trial, former Saskatchewan cabinet minister Colin Thatcher was found guilty of the first-degree murder of his ex-wife JoAnn Wilson. His appeal for a new trial was rejected.

Right: Dr. Henry Morgentaler, surrounded by anti-abortion protesters, leaves a Toronto courtroom after a judge had upheld his release from jail on bail with no conditions in 1983. Morgentaler had been charged with performing abortions at his Toronto clinic. His clinics in Montreal, Winnipeg and Toronto became the focus of the abortion debate in Canada.

Left: Alex Baumann, Canada's swimming champion, winning one of his two gold medals at the 1984 Los Angeles Olympics. Baumann is one of only four Canadians to have won two gold medals at the games.

Pope John Paul II's triumphant visit to Canada in 1984 included a few precious moments of quiet reflection. Saying his rosary, the Pope strolls along a path in Elk Island National Park, east of Edmonton.

This 1984 photograph could have been taken during the Depression. Floyd Riviere, a farmer near Pincher Creek, Alberta, looks at parched land that was once a watering hole for his cattle. Many farmers and cattlemen have gone bankrupt buying emergency feed for their cattle at exorbitant prices.

Québécois novelist Jacques Ferron founded the Rhinoceros Party in 1972 as an outlet for frustrated voters who wished to register a protest vote against the platforms (or lack thereof) of the registered parties. Over the years, the Rhinoceros Party gained amazing popularity and soon it was sporting candidates across the country. The platforms were always deliberately silly and it was the party's policy never to get a candidate elected. When Ferron died in 1985, the Rhinoceros Party disbanded itself in his honour.

Above left: Jeanne Sauvé is accompanied by Opposition Leader Joe Clark and Prime Minister Pierre Trudeau as she takes her place as the first woman Speaker of the House at the opening of Parliament in 1980. In 1984, she set a precedent again when she was sworn in as Canada's first female governor general.

Below left: Pierre Trudeau adopts his famous gunslinger pose while thousands cheer him at the Liberal leadership convention of 1984. It was at this convention that Trudeau stepped down as leader of the federal Liberals.

Right: The world's favourite royal couple, the Prince and Princess of Wales, Charles and Diana, pose in Victorian dress in Edmonton during their 1985 royal tour of Canada. Diana dazzled onlookers with her designer clothing, quite a fashion change for the Royal Family.

Former teacher Jim Keegstra (left) and his lawyer Doug Christie talk to reporters on the steps of the Red Deer courthouse where Keegstra stood trial for wilfully promoting hatred against Jews. He was convicted of this charge at the end of a long and sensational trial.

Right: Reshaw Cheema (left) is comforted by Dilraj Cheema as she mourns the death of her son in the crash of Air India Flight 182 that exploded in mid-air off the coast of Ireland in June, 1985. Most of the passengers aboard were Canadian citizens. The crash has been linked to the explosion of a bomb believed to have been placed by Sikh extremists.

Left: Firemen turn hoses on the burning wreckage after a VIA Rail passenger train collided with a CN freight train near Hinton, Alberta, on February 8, 1986. Thirty-three people died after being trapped and crushed in the twisted wreckage. An inquiry concluded that the CN freight crew caused the accident when they failed to divert their train to a siding to let the passenger cars pass. All the CN crew perished except for one crew member who was at the back of the train.

One of Canada's worst aircraft tragedies took place near Gander, Newfoundland, on December 12, 1985, when a DC8 chartered plane carrying American servicemen home for Christmas crashed after takeoff. All of the more than two hundred men aboard were killed.

Above: Shawn O'Sullivan, Canada's welter-weight boxer, wins by a knockout in the second round against Alberto Lopez of Mexico in Dartmouth, Nova Scotia, on March 27, 1986.

Left: In the wake of Terry Fox, Steve Fonyo began his own marathon run across Canada to raise funds for cancer research. Fonyo, also a cancer victim amputee, successfully completed his run and is seen here at the conclusion of his run, pouring water from the Atlantic Ocean into the Pacific Ocean at Victoria on May 29, 1985.

Right: Vancouver's Expo 86 is the smash hit of the year. One of the features of the fair is on-site entertainment taking place all over the festival site. Here, costumed figures perform before Expo's landmark dome, Expo Centre. This strawman character startled Diana, Princess of Wales as he approached her during the official royal tour of the fair.

Photo Credits

CBC, 70-71 (top), 85, 105
Calgary Herald, (Kent Stevenson), 103; 182
Canada-Wide/*Toronto Sun;* 18, 56, 57, 72,
 74, 76, 94, 95, 99, 121, 122, 136-37, 164
Canada's Sports Hall of Fame/CNE, 60
CanaPress, 21 (top), 22, 24, 27, 31, 33;
 (DND), 37; 39, 42, 45; (DND), 46, 49
 (top); (NS Archives), 49 (bottom); 55, 62,
 70, 75, 86; *(The Chronicle-Herald),* 88;
 89, 90, 92-93, 100, 101, 102, 104, 106,
 107, 108, 109, 110, 116, 117, 118, 125,
 128, 129, 130, 131, 133, 134, 140, 142,
 143, 144, 146, 147, 148, 151, 157, 158,
 159, 160; *(Chicoutimi Le Quotidien),* 165;
 166, 167 (bottom), 170, 171, 173, 175
 (bottom), 177, 180, 181, 183, 184, 189,
 190 (bottom)
City of Toronto Archives/*Globe and Mail*
 Collection, (148364-X), 68-69
Walter Curtin, 145
Edmonton Journal, 98 (top), 168
Edmonton Sun, 188
Glenbow Archives, Calgary, Alberta, 32
The Globe and Mail, (55231-1), 51; (54089-
 2), 73; (Harold Robinson), 77, 84; 111; (J.
 Allan Moffatt/67157-83), 120; (Barrie
 Davis/70077-05), 127; 156; (Thomas
 Szlukovenyi), 176; (Zoran Milich/36A),
 190
Hockey Hall of Fame and Museum, 61,
 64-65
La Presse, 79 (top), 138-39
Le Journal de Québec, 167 (top)
Franz Maier, 123, 126
News of the North, 155
Public Archives of Canada, (C. Dettloff/
 PAC/C 38723), 6; (PAC/PA 119013),
 11; (Man/PAC/PA 145949), 15; (Air
 Canada/PAC/C 84023), 20;
 (CBC/PAC/C 27901), 21 (bottom);
 (NFB/PAC/PA 116874), 23; (A.C.

Kells/PAC/PA 116362), 25; (PAC/PA
 119765), 26; (NFB/PAC/C 24452), 28
 (top); (DND/PAC/PA 37467), 28
 (bottom); (Milne Studios Ltd./PAC/C
 29452), 29; (PAC/C 25), 30; (PAC/C
 14160), 34; (Frederick G. Whitcombe/
 DND/PAC/PA 141311), 35; (Frank
 Royal/DND/PAC/PA 37479), 36;
 (Montreal Gazette/PAC/C 14168), 38;
 (G. Milne/DND/PAC/PA 122765), 40-
 41; (Bell/DND/PAC/PA 132839), 43;
 (A.M. Stirton/PAC/PA 113697), 44;
 (NFB/PAC/PA 113697), 48; (Frank
 Royal/NFB/PAC/PA 112691), 54:
 (NFB/PAC/PA 128080), 58;
 (TCA/PAC/PA 143523), 59;
 (NFB/PAC/C 85040), 63; (MacLean/
 DND/PAC/C 79009), 66; (PAC/C
 90482), 81; (D. Cameron/PAC/C 94168,
 87; (PAC/PA 150429), 90-91 (top);
 (Centennial Commission/PAC/C 5306),
 113; (B. Cadzow/PAC/PA 115203), 119
Mrs. Dawn Attis/Public Archives of Nova
 Scotia, 78
Ontario Archives, (S. 801), 19
Robert Ragsdale, 79 (top), 98 (bottom)
Red Deer Advocate, 186
Regina Leader-Post, 178
Saskatchewan Archives Board, (R-B2895),
 47
Peter Timmermans, 191
The Toronto Star, 16, 85-86, 135, 149, 161,
 162-3, 179, 185, 190 (top)
Vancouver Province, 97, 141, 154, 169, 175
 (top)
Vancouver Public Library, (1294), 17
Vancouver Sun, (Len Erlundson), 92; 96;
 (Glen Baglo), 132; 174; (Greg Kinch),187
Winnipeg Tribune, 67
York University/*Toronto Telegram*
 Collection, 124